Population 85

The Story of a Small Town in Northern California

Battle Creek Meadows

Population 85
The Story of a Small Town in Northern California

Jo Ann Beresford Perkins

STANSBURY
PUBLISHING
Chico, Ca.

FRONT COVER
Mineral from Turner Mountain Lookout with Brokeoff Mountain
and Lassen Peak in the background

HALF TITLE PAGE
Top: Roadside welcome sign (Jo Ann Perkins)

BACK COVER
Graphics from Mineral Lodge brochure, c. 1950s

FRONTISPIECE
Battle Creek Meadows, c. 2016 (Josie Smith)

Unless otherwise noted, all photographs featured in this book are
from the collection of Jo Ann Perkins

Map from Mineral Lodge brochure, c. 1950s
Map inset adapted from Google Maps

Copyright © 2018 by Jo Ann Beresford Perkins
All rights reserved. Printed in the United States of America

ISBN: 978-1-935807-42-1
Library of Congress Control Number: 2018939707

Layout and design by Josie Reifschneider-Smith
Stansbury Publishing is an imprint of Heidelberg Graphics

Dedication

This book is dedicated to all of the people who came to Mineral,
from the night watchman at Diamond National in Red Bluff
to the president of Standard Oil of California
from San Francisco.

This exposure to many different people allowed me to grow up
and live my life with a good understanding of the world
and to appreciate all of its people.

This deer head, which hangs in the Mill Creek Resort restaurant, is similar to the ones that lined the front porches of both Mineral Lodges. (courtesy Mill Creek Resort)

~ Table of Contents ~

Dedication v
Preface ix
Acknowledgments xi
Map xiii

Chapter 1
 Early History 1

Adventure in Ishi Country 5

Chapter 2
 Early Settlers and the Tehama County Wagon Road 9

Chapter 3
 Woodson and Beresford 17

Chapter 4
 My Family 27

My Mother's Wedding 43

Chapter 5
 Growing Up in Mineral 45

Chapter 6
 The Mineral Lodges 57

Chapter 7
 The Store 73

Chapter 8
 The Coffee Shop 85

Holidays 95

Chapter 9
 The Gift Shop 99

Edythe 105

Chapter 10
    The Buffet 109

Betty Brown 119

Chapter 11
    Cabins 121

Chapter 12
    Garage and Service Station 127

Chapter 13
    The Subdivisions 131

Chapter 14
    The Mineral School 135

The Mineral Mill 142
Mineral Hose Company No. 1 146

Chapter 15
    Skiing 149

Chapter 16
    Lassen Volcanic National Park 163

Spice 177

Chapter 17
    Mountain Lookouts 181
    Robert Harvey Abbey 186

Ardith 189

Chapter 18
    The CCC Camp 195

Lost 198

Chapter 19
    Minke 201

About the Author 204

~ Preface ~

When the temperature drops to someplace around 15-20 degrees Fahrenheit, all the water in small, shallow puddles turns to ice and when stepped on makes a wonderful cracking noise and splinters into a million ice particles. From October through March, my younger brother, Fred, and I delighted in this ritual every morning as we walked to school. The puddles were larger and deeper around the Standard Oil Service Station. If the temperature was warmer and it had rained, there was no ice so we just waded through, hoping the water would not go over our boots. If it had snowed, the puddles were deceptive and gave us a greater challenge to keep our feet dry. Most of the time it was ice and more ice, and we raced to see who could get to the bigger puddles first.

West of the service station on State Highway 36 was a regular highway sign that read, "MINERAL, pop. 85." This described the small town where I grew up and thence the title of this book. Mineral was, and still is, best characterized as a "WIDE SPOT IN THE ROAD." But it was a magical place to me as a child. It had a special feeling for me then, and it still does now, even though I have not lived there permanently for over 30 years.

Mineral is located in Northern California approximately 100 miles south of the border with Oregon and 150 miles from the eastern border with Nevada. It sits in a lovely mountain meadow at an altitude of 4,950 feet. This pleasant meadow is ringed by mountains covered with evergreens. Ponderosa pines at heights of well over 100 feet, interspersed with white firs and incense cedar, tower over the landscape. The climate at this elevation is delightful in the summer months with temperatures of 75-80 degrees Fahrenheit. Winters can be severe with an abundance of rain and snow storms, rewarded by clearing skies of brilliant sun. The sky is usually a deep azure blue, giving way to a sparkling Milky Way after dark.

The southern entrance to Lassen Volcanic National Park is only nine miles from Mineral. Lassen Peak was the only active volcano in the United States when it erupted in the spring of 1914. Congress designated it as a National Park in 1916. The mountain was still smoking when I was in my teens but is still considered an active volcano. There is considerable volcanic activity, with boiling mud pots and steam vents to make it an interesting place to visit. Lassen Park is considered one of the hidden gems in our National Park system with its many alpine lakes and miles of hiking trails.

With its proximity to the Park and a delightful climate, Mineral is truly a resort area, and its resort is the Mineral Lodge. My family owned and operated this business for sixty years. I was fortunate to be able live most of my life in this "WIDE SPOT IN THE ROAD."

Jo Ann Beresford Perkins

∽ Acknowledgements ∽

This book would never have been written if it would not have been for the Salvation Army office in Red Bluff.

I moved to Lincoln Sun City in the fall of 2001 where I enjoyed skiing and hiking until I fell and broke my hip. Since I was unable to move easily, I decided to move to Mineral and write the book I had always thought about writing. So I moved to Red Bluff and wrote the first page.

And that was it for about two years.

Luckily, I discovered the Salvation Army writing group. This group had been established years before for seniors to write their memories and was held every week at the Army's office on Walnut Street.

The Salvation Army provided coffee for the group of 10 or 12 people who read aloud what they had written the week before. Ray Dunn, who was a talented writer, headed the group. There was no coaching, instructions, or critique of your work, but there was great encouragement. Ray would hand your work back the next week with little typewritten notes with colorful stickers on them. I now treasure the only three examples that I saved.

This group no longer exists. Ray passed away about 10 years ago, and we carried on for a few more years, but I am sure all of us look back on those meetings with pleasure of the time spent. Not only did I make good friends, but I wrote this books!

I owe a debt of gratitude to Gene Serr and Maggi Milton for proofreading this book; Dan Foster, Beverly Ogle, W. L. Stillwell, Frank McCaughey, Floy Woodward, Joel Rienhard, Betty Brown, Tina Jones, and Josh Dale for graciously allowing photographs from their collections to be used in this book; Hobart Moulton and his book *We Are Not Forgotten*; and Josie Smith for a superior job of editing.

> *Mineral has much for people who love the outdoors—hiking, fishing, hunting, and other outdoor sports. Your continuing saga of Mineral and its inhabitants is interesting and informative. This is the way history should be written.*
>
> ~ *Ray Dunn*

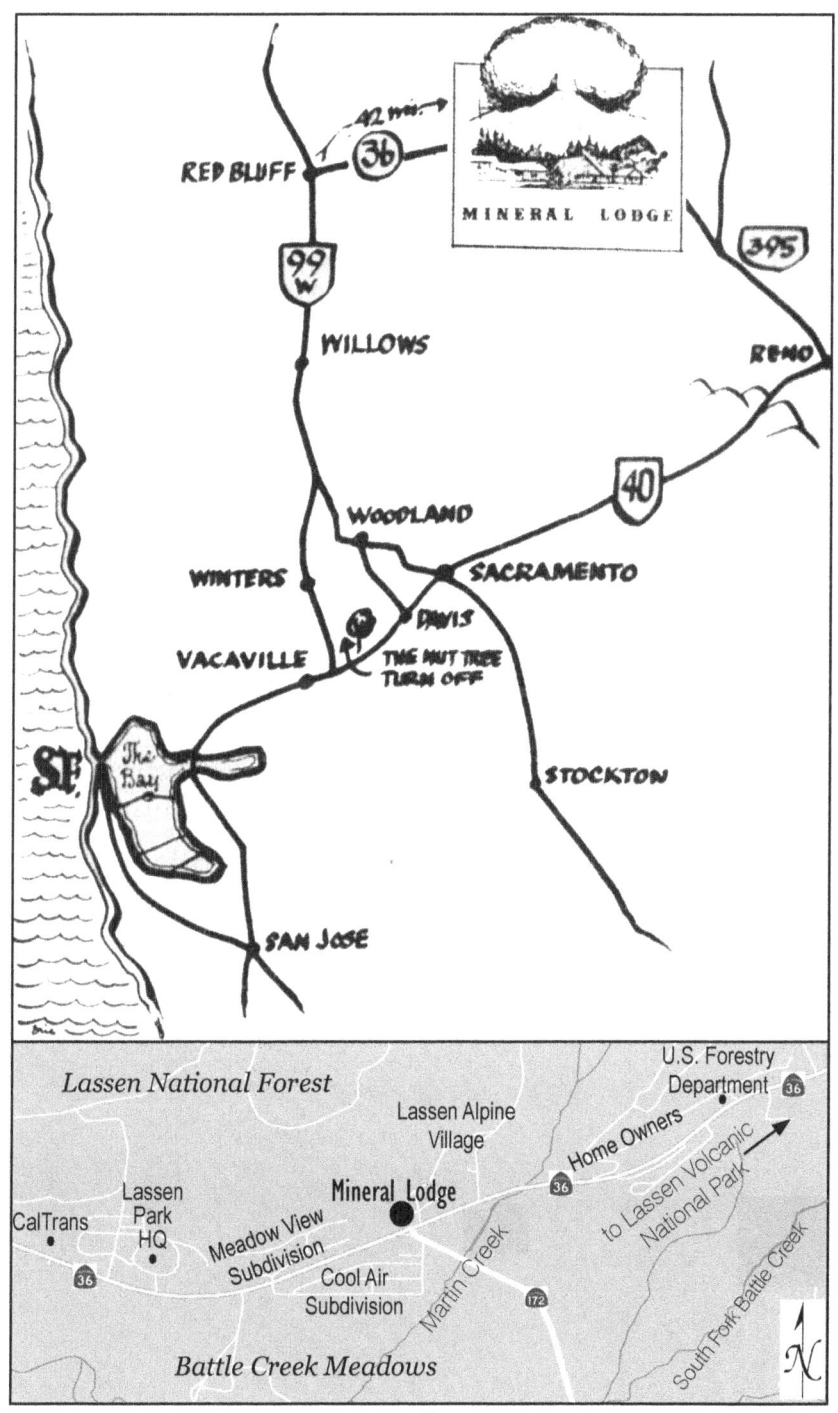

Projectile points found over the years in the Mineral area by the author

CHAPTER 1

EARLY HISTORY

The first people in the Mineral area were the Indians. The Yahi Indians, a sub-tribe of the Yana, lived mainly in the isolated canyons of Mill Creek and Deer Creek located 10-20 miles southwest of Mineral at the 3,000 feet elevation. In the summer months, the Indians migrated to the mountain meadows to escape the heat. They followed the migrating black-tailed deer and fished in the clear streams for rainbow trout. I have a collection of small arrowheads that I found when I was growing up, but many larger points and even spearheads have been found in and around Mineral.

"The Mill Creeks," as the Yahi were called by the early settlers in the Sacramento Valley, never assimilated with the newly arrived immigrants. They stole horses and cattle and generally terrorized the settlers, always escaping up to the rugged country they called home. A concentrated effort to eliminate these troublesome Indians was successful in 1864 when the majority were driven into Kingsley Cave above Mill Creek where most were annihilated. The few survivors never caused any more trouble and had a hard time feeding themselves with so few left to hunt. In 1911 the last surviving Yahi Indian was found starving beside a slaughterhouse in Oroville. The sheriff put him in the jail for safekeeping. No one

Mill Creek

could understand his language, and no one knew quite what to do with him until A. L. Kroeber and T. T. Waterman, anthropologists from the University of California at Berkeley, stepped forward and agreed to be responsible for his care. He was given a room in the university museum in San Francisco and even received a small salary. He was given the name of "Ishi" that means man in his own language. Due to his association with the professors, he left us a rich heritage of California Indian life of his particular tribe. He was a gentle man and enjoyed his life in the museum, made many friends, and loved riding the cable cars. Unfortunately, he lived less than five more years because he had no natural immunity from our diseases, and he died of tuberculosis. Ishi's cremated body was buried in a cemetery near San Francisco, but his brain was shipped to the Smithsonian Institute in Washington, D. C. for study. Local Maidu Indians in the Sacramento Valley persuaded the Smithsonian to release the brain. It was united with his body and buried in a secret location in 2000.

To learn more about this interesting story, you can read Ishi in *Two Worlds* written by Theodora Kroeber, A. L. Kroeber's widow. There are several other books concerning Ishi, but I think this is the best one.

In the heart of Ishi country is Black Rock, a large, basalt rock formation on Mill Creek. On the Old Lassen Trail above this formation sits the Ishi Marker, placed here in 2007 by the Redding Rancheria Ishi Conservation Group to honor a final chapter of his life. As a child, Beverly Ogle, who spearheaded this project, had imagined that the face of Ishi should be carved on Black Rock. She also felt that Ishi himself had probably walked on the river rock that was used for the project.

The Ishi Marker is made from washed river rock found along Mill Creek with an etched bronze plaque of the bust of Ishi looking toward the sky. It sits on the Narrows that separates Mill Creek and Deer Creek canyons. The Narrows is a small strip of land that made a hazardous roadbed for the pioneers traveling with Peter Lassen on his trail west. Parts of this trail are still visible in the area. Black Rock can be reached via Ponderosa Way, a narrow, unpaved, county road between Hwy 36 and Hwy 32. It is an interesting trip that crosses the south and north forks of Antelope Creek then plunges into austere Mill Creek Canyon. The area is wild and remote, giving a bird's eye view of what life must have been like for the Yahi Indians. Four-wheel drive is recommended.

For many centuries, the Indians enjoyed peace and quiet during their summers in Mineral's mountain meadows until they were invaded by trappers and explorers from the late 1820s to the early 1840s. In his 1990 article in Tehama County Genealogical & Historical Society's *Memories*, Dan Foster states that Peter Skene Ogden from the Hudson's Bay Company passed through the area in 1827. Foster also states that when W. E. Gerber purchased Battle Creek Meadows in 1894 from Henry Wilson, for whom Wilson Lake is named, there was an old cabin with an engraving on the wall that read "Hudson Bay Company." I had never heard this before, however, Dan Foster is and has been the local caretaker of the Battle Creek Meadows property for several years.

In reading a copy of an interview with D. B. Lyon of Red Bluff, taken in 1945 by Lassen Park Naturalist Harry B. Robinson,

Ishi Monument (courtesy Beverly Ogle)

I found the following information: Mr. Lyon, who had been a rider for cattlemen throughout the Mineral area, stated that when he came into Battle Creek Meadows (the original name given Mineral) for the first time in 1880, there was a lone, log cabin in the meadows. He remembers seeing names and initials, many in French.

I found credible evidence to support the idea that Ogden and the Hudson's Bay Company might have been in the area in Robert Utley's *A Life Wild and Perilous*. The book states that Ewing Young, an early trapper looking for beaver, encountered Peter Skene Ogden heading a brigade of 60 Hudson's Bay trappers in California. The two groups worked together trapping beaver down the San Joaquin River and up the Sacramento River nearly to the mountains. The year was 1830. With Ogden's 60 men plus Ewing's group, they may well have followed Battle Creek, which flows into the Sacramento River north of Red Bluff from the Mineral area. A further indication of their presence is the fact that, around 1975, beaver had a pond in the upper Battle Creek Meadows.

ADVENTURE IN ISHI COUNTRY

I have trekked in Nepal and slept in a headhunter's lodge in Borneo, but the highest adventure I ever had took place only 20 miles from Mineral in Mill Creek Canyon. This was part of the home territory for Ishi where he was able to live undetected for several years because of the topography and remoteness of the area. It is much the same today as it was then. Mill Creek's headwaters begin in Lassen Park and flow eventually into the Sacramento River near Los Molinos. My dear friend Minki Brown was fascinated with the area around Black Rock and spent lots of time exploring it. She discovered a cave above Mill Creek and loved to spend time there with her family.

One Easter vacation, she suggested that her fellow teacher, Chuck Kindig, and I come with her. As the two of us did not want to spend a whole week there, Chuck and I decided to come by ourselves later in the week. It was possible to drive so far and then hike to the cave, which is what Minki did; however, Chuck was unsure of the route and was afraid we might get lost. The Ponderosa Way, an unpaved road, crosses Mill Creek at Black Rock where there is a trail going east and west along the stream. Chuck and I decided to go in this way to meet Minki. We knew it was more than a day's hike to the cave, so we were prepared to spend the night on the trail. I had a beautiful, new, lightweight sleeping bag and backpack. We had packed plenty of food for our trip since we planned to stay two days at the cave and then return home with Minki. We had another friend drop us off at Black Rock. Minki and I had hiked often from the Hole-in-the-Ground Campground near Mill Creek Resort to Black Rock, a distance of 20 miles. Once you started hiking, there was no way out except up or down the trail because of the steepness of the terrain. The trail Chuck and I planned to take was much the same. I had never been on the trail west of Black Rock so was looking forward to this new experience.

The first day's walk was wonderful, the trail was mostly downhill, the weather was fair and balmy, and we were having a good time. We camped at the Papy place, an abandoned homestead with unlivable structures and unused gardens. This was according to schedule—we planned to join Minki by the next afternoon. We were able to walk along the stream most of the next morning and had lunch with our feet in the water with bright sunshine all around. It was peaceful and quiet except for the gurgling of the water. We knew there was no one else close by, but the cave and our friend were just down the trail.

After lunch the terrain became much steeper, and the trail climbed up the side of the hill so we could no longer see the creek. Suddenly the trail disappeared because of a landslide area. In order to continue, we had to jump down a three to four foot drop of loose dirt. I expressed fear of not being able to negotiate this maneuver with my heavy backpack. Chuck suggested that I remove it, toss it down, and jump down after it. This did not work as well as planned because the backpack rolled quite a ways down in the loose soil and stopped about three feet from a drop off into Mill Creek. How far down to the stream I will never know. It seemed too dangerous to try to retrieve my backpack, but, as I was saying this, Chuck started toward it, slipped, and slid on his back moving fast toward the edge. Before I realized what was happening, he rolled over and grabbed a small bush with one outstretched hand, thus saving himself from going over the edge. With a lot of effort he was able to pull himself up until he could crawl back to where I stood. My backpack was still in the same position. At this point, we were both quite shaken and decided to leave the backpack where it was. Fortunately, we had split up the food, so we felt we could get along with what was in his pack, and, of course, Minki had enough supplies in the cave.

All I could think of was to get away from this dangerous area near the stream, so we started up this very steep hill through trees and poison oak until we reached a level area high above the creek; we could not see the opposite bank easily from this vantage point. We continued to walk west hoping we would find Minki and her cave. Actually we never did find it, probably because of the steep banks of both Mill Creek and its tributaries. Around four in the afternoon we knew we were too far west for the cave. We felt we should camp for the night and try again the next day, but there was no level place to camp near the creek because of the terrain. After another hour or so in a westward direction, we found a tributary with a rather rocky, level spot. The camp stove was in Chuck's pack, so we had a nice hot meal and settled down for the night in one sleeping bag with as few rocks under us as possible.

It was raining lightly when we awoke in the morning. After a hurried cold breakfast we decided our best option was to go back toward Black Rock where we had started, hoping to find Minki on the way. We were probably within 12 miles of Los Molinos if we continued west, but had no way back to Mineral from there. After a few hours of light rain it cleared up, and we felt better about the world. We saw one puff of smoke as we were walking east. It must have come from the cave, but we were unable to pinpoint the location, and there was no more smoke. About three in the afternoon we reached the Papy place where we had camped the first night. We stopped, cooked a hot meal, then continued up the trail until about an hour before dark where we decided to camp for the night. We considered walking in the dark to get to Black Rock but felt it would be too dangerous at night because the trail was high and narrow above the water.

In the meantime the clouds had thickened, and it looked like rain again. We built a roaring fire, rigged up a tarp for shelter against the rain, and dug a trench around where we planned to sleep to drain the water away from us.

With a crack of lightening the rain came down so hard the fire was out instantly. We crawled into the sleeping bag, hoped the rain would let up, some miracle might happen, and we would wake up in bright sunshine. After about two hours, the water started seeping under the sleeping bag, It got a lot colder, and the rain continued, only much more intensely. Thinking we might be frozen by morning, we got up, packed up all the gear, and headed back up the trail in the rain. Our only assets were a waterproof map of the trail and a large flashlight that had luckily been in the bottom of Chuck's pack.

We knew that there might be some sort of shelter at Hugh and Lorena Hulseman's about half a mile below Black Rock. No one had been there two days before, but we hoped they might be home, or that we could find some sort of shelter. The trail was wet and slippery, and I walked behind Chuck with the flashlight so we could both see the trail. At one point I saw a fresh mountain lion track in the trail. I never said a word, just hoped the animal was not interested in us.

We walked for nearly four hours before we reached the Hulseman's and could see by a light in the windows that someone was home. By this time we, and everything we had, was drenched. The Hulsemans were Maidu Indians, and we knew it was dangerous to just walk up to their door because they might feel threatened at that hour with their remote location. I hoped that Lorena would remember my father, so I started shouting for help saying, "I am Husky Beresford's daughter." It really sounded silly but seemed the best approach considering the circumstances. Hugh finally came outside, and we were invited in. Walking across the pasture area had been terrible because we had sunk up to our thighs in holes, and it had still been raining hard. We dripped cascades as we entered their living room at 2:00 a.m.

After we explained who we were and why we were there, Lorena got over the shock of having uninvited guests, made us a bed before the fireplace, lent us dry clothing to sleep in, and hung our wet ones to dry. It was nice to be dry, feel the warm fire, and, best of all, to feel safe and sound.

The next morning Lorena cooked us a wonderful breakfast of homemade biscuits, home-cured ham, eggs, and pancakes. This really made us feel like we had landed in heaven. She even drove us home to Mineral because the telephone service was out due to the storm, and there was no way to contact anyone to pick us up.

I never saw my sleeping bag and backpack again, I still don't know where the cave is, but I am glad to be alive. To this day, I still wake up at night and wonder what I ever would have done if Chuck had fallen over that edge. There was no one to call and no one to help. We did not even have a rope with us.

CHAPTER 2

Early Settlers and the Tehama County Wagon Road

The Mineral area was referred to as Battle Creek Meadows by early settlers. Hiram Rawson and his brother Cyrus drove sheep to the area in 1860 looking for green grass to feed livestock in the summer months. They built a cabin and some corrals. They later gained title to the land under the Swamp and Overflow Act in which Congress gave free title to land if a boat could be rowed around it; no mention was made of water for the boat. The story goes that the Rawsons put a small row boat on a spring wagon and drove the perimeter of the property they wanted to acquire; one of them rowed the boat while the other managed the wagon. Several other mountain meadows were acquired using this method.

Mineral would not exist today if it were not for State Highway 36 that runs east and west between Fortuna and Susanville. This route began as a system of trails that branched off from the two famous trails to Northern California—Lassen Trail and Nobles Trail. The Nobles Trail took wagon trains from Humboldt in Nevada through Susanville, north around Cinder Cone, and then west to Old Shasta. The Lassen Trail guided travelers north near Alturas, south through present day Lake Almanor to the head of Deer Creek, and

Battle Creek Meadows with Turner Mountain

then west to the Sacramento River. It did not take long for some travelers to figure out that they could save many miles by leaving the Nobles Trail at Susanville and go to the head of Deer Creek, then east through Childs Meadow over Mineral Summit to Mineral at the head of Battle Creek, down the south side of Battle Creek Canyon to Paynes Creek, north around Inskip Butte, and west to the mouth of Battle Creek at the Sacramento River.

Red Bluff became an important hub, warehousing and transporting goods north and east for the Gold Rush. There were few good roads in 1853, and rivers were easier for transporting goods. Red Bluff was as far north as the river boats could navigate due to China Rapids above Red Bluff. Business was booming, especially when new silver mines were discovered in the Nevada Territory. Competition arose when General Bidwell developed the Chico-Humboldt wagon road from Chico Landing to Susanville, which at that time was in Nevada Territory.

Walston Chalmers, editor and publisher of the *Red Bluff Independent*, realized his town was losing business and began to lobby through his newspaper to improve the existing trail to the east. Due to his efforts and the backing of Nevada's governor, Isaac Roop, a $40,000 bond issue was passed on February 10, 1863. Work began immediately, and the road, dubbed The Tehama County Wagon Road, was officially declared completed on September 22 of that same year with few changes from the original trail system. The main change was starting from Red Bluff instead of the mouth of Battle Creek. A stage line, the Humboldt Stage, advertised a fare of $50 for the 7-8 day trip, which included meals.

The Tehama County Wagon Road established stations along its route to facilitate travel. Each station had a blacksmith shop and a stable; some had a place to sleep and served food. The first station from Red Bluff was 14 miles out named Dale's Station; then came the Hickman place at Paynes Creek; and on to Mineral, where John Burgess had a hotel and a toll bridge across Battle Creek. Tolls were charged to help with the upkeep of the road. In 1864, the toll ran from $1 for a man and his horse to $10 for an eight-horse team. Loose stock was 16 cents per head for cattle and 10 cents per head for hogs and sheep. J. C. Tyler, who owned what is now Childs Meadow, was appointed agent for the road by the Tehama County supervisors. His job was to collect tolls, repair and maintain the road, and also keep it open during the winter months. Snows were much deeper then; the winter of 1899 received 21 feet of snow at Mineral. You wonder how Tyler kept the road open in the winter months.

With good access to the mountains, people in the Sacramento Valley began to discover the wonderful climate in the higher elevations. Malaria was present in the valley, and it was extremely hot with no air conditioning or electric fans. It took two days by horse and wagon from Red Bluff, but people flocked to the meadow areas of Mill Creek and Battle Creek for the summer months. Some built cabins; others just camped. The first public business in Battle Creek Meadows was opened by W. S. Ranford in 1865. He advertised that his place of business had a good supply of groceries, fruits and vegetables, cigars, and liquors. That same year, J. McLaughlin advertised a summer school for children of families in the area. The *Red Bluff Independent* reported that 150 to 200 people had spent the summer months luxuriating in the cool mountain air of Battle Creek and Mill Creek Meadows. Harry Burrichter advertised that he could supply the best quality clear ice, eight inches thick, available from Battle Creek Meadows for eight cents per pound.

Bert Hampton, originally from Michigan, homesteaded 160 acres along Martin Creek in 1894. Later he acquired additional land for a total of 480 acres. In the beginning, he sold hay to travelers, building a large barn for this purpose in 1898. He had one of the first hotels in the area, a two-story home near his barn. Hampton soon realized the potential for business as he subsequently built a general store and what was referred to as a cook shack a short distance west of the house.

A post office with the name of Mineral Springs had been established on property owned by the Morgan family in Mill Creek Meadows for the people camping there for the summer months. When the

Hampton Hotel

Morgan family sold the land, people were no longer welcome to camp there, so they moved the camps to the Mineral area. The post office moved with them. Only the name of "Mineral" continued to be used because there are no springs in the area. This is how Mineral received its name—before then the area was referred to as Hampton's or Battle Creek Meadows. Bert Hampton became the first postmaster in present-day Mineral in 1902. He also built several cabins for travelers. A few of these cabins are still standing today. Hobart Moulton remembered sleeping in the hayloft in Hampton's barn on one occasion and renting a cabin for sleeping another time. They obtained water from a ditch that came from Martin Creek. Evidence remains of these ditches today.

Bert Hampton had two sons, Elbert and Olen. Both of these men were alive in my childhood and had cabins on the property. Elbert lost a leg in a railroad accident and made his own wooden one; he also canned his own meat. He ran cattle in the Mineral area on a Forest Service permit, bringing them up from Lanes Valley only in the summer months. He was famous for fixing everything with

The hotel became Warren Woodson's summer home. The author grew up here.

Hampton barn burning

baling wire, the thin wire used for baling hay. There is a humorous story concerning Elbert. He was deer hunting with my father and others in the Paynes Creek area when he accidently shot one of the horses. He never stopped shooting at the deer, shouting, "I shot your horse Husky!" Bang! Bang! Bang! This horse had a bad habit of rearing and apparently reared at the wrong time.

Olen, the younger son, climbed Lassen Peak on his 80th birthday. He had worked for Lassen Park maintaining this trail in his youth; he was sure he had climbed the peak at least 50 times. He said he used to climb it without a trail in 30 minutes, and he remembered where he had seen his first bear. At 80 years old it took him four hours, but he made it to the summit.

Emil Gerber purchased what is now the Battle Creek Meadows Ranch in 1894. He originally came from New York and was president of the California National Bank in Sacramento. In 1899, with partner Will Conard, Gerber brought 42 purebred Hereford cows and two bulls from England, driving them to the meadows at Mineral for summer pasture. He abandoned this project later as he could not keep the stray bulls out due to poor fencing of the land. In 1900, Gerber erected a sawmill to provide lumber for fences, corrals, barns, and houses that he subsequently built on the property. One grand, two-story home was built for his family of five children with an octagon gazebo. These buildings still stand today. Upon his death, two of his daughters purchased the property, and their descendants still own and operate the ranch. The ranch is over 2,000 acres, most of it in meadow land. The Leninger family has leased the meadows as summer range for their cattle since the early 1940s. The original lease was consummated with a hand shake. The Gerber descendants use the ranch for vacationing with a caretaker to oversee the property when they are absent.

In 1910, Gerber formed the Tehama Investment Company and filed the plat for the town of Gerber. He never lived there, but it is his namesake. With a friend, he was in the first car driven from Red Bluff to Mineral in 1907. Realizing that automobiles would make the trip to the ranch easier, he purchased a seven-passenger, 60-HP Pierce Arrow that was used thereafter to take the family from the train station in Red Bluff to the ranch in Mineral.

A. L. Conard, who operated the Tremont Hotel in Red Bluff, purchased some 12 acres at the upper end of Battle Creek Meadows sometime in the early 1900s. The property had a sulphur-type spring that was sometimes used for curative purposes. Descendants of the Conard family still own the property today.

Lassen National Forest was established in 1905. Any land not privately owned in the Mineral area was included. These federal lands were under the Department of Agriculture and encompassed some 12,000 acres. The main office was first located in Red Bluff; summer headquarters was moved to Mineral in 1909. The summer headquarters was located one mile east of Hampton's store and consisted of three two-bedroom homes, a bunk house, and three large garages or warehouses. Robert Harvey Abbey was employed as a ranger for the Forest Service during this time. He left a wonderful diary describing his activities during his employment from 1905-1920. During the winter of 1910-11, he made frequent visits to Mineral from Red Bluff to shovel snow off the roofs of the buildings. He rode in the U. S. Mail stage to Paynes Creek then walked the remaining 19 miles, the last six or seven miles on skis or snowshoes because the snow depths were sometimes close to 11 feet. You will hear of Abbey again as he was the first person to look into the crater of Lassen Peak after it first erupted in 1914.

Lassen National Forest still has facilities in Mineral, open only in the summer months. Today the main office is located in Susanville with a district office in Chester. ✥

Rainbow trout (Eastman Studio)

CHAPTER 3

WOODSON AND BERESFORD

Warren Woodson and Fred G. (Grant) Beresford purchased the 480 acres that encompassed most of Mineral from Bert Hampton in 1920. Beresford was my paternal grandfather, and Warren Woodson was his employer and friend. The people from the town of Corning were a great support system for Mineral—purchasing lots on which to build summer homes, frequenting the area to escape the summer heat, staying several days and eating in the restaurant or purchasing groceries from the store. I feel that Warren Woodson and the story of Corning deserve more telling because it is interesting and a great part in the history of Mineral.

Woodson, who is considered the "Father of Corning," is a wonderful example of a self-made man. He was born in Sacramento in 1863 and grew up in Fresno where he dropped out of school after the fourth grade to help support his mother, brother, and two sisters. He picked acorns, herded sheep, and tended hogs, among other jobs. When his mother moved the family to Red Bluff to be near her parents, he washed dishes and waited tables at the Tremont Hotel for 75 cents a day. At age 16 he went to work for the Sierra Lumber Company where he became a bookkeeper. He then worked as a clerk for the general store of Clark and Mayhew and was the postmaster for the town of Red Bluff for four years beginning in

Warren Woodson

1886. During all this time, he spent many hours reading anything and everything.

As postmaster, Woodson received many letters from people inquiring about small plots of land to purchase. This gave him the idea to develop land for this purpose. He became associated with Charles F. Foster who had been a senator in the State legislature and Sheriff of Tehama County. In 1891, they purchased 3,107 acres in and around Corning for a price of $77,675. They chose the name "The Maywood Colony" after a suburb in Chicago. This was the beginning of a large subdivision that eventually contained more than 40,000 acres. At that time, Corning was only 161 acres and was owned by the Central Pacific Railroad. George Hoag had sold the 161 acres to the railroad on the condition that they build a

Fred G. Beresford

depot and passenger station so trains would stop and that they lay out a town site with lots to sell.

Woodson went east to promote the sale of his 10-acre parcels. His advertising offered "good fruit land" between one and two miles from the Corning railroad station for $5.50 down and $1.37 per acre for 36 months. Land nearer to the depot sold for $8 down and $2 per month. He established offices in Boston, Chicago, and New York. For an additional small payment, Woodson offered to plant, maintain, and harvest fruit orchards on the purchased land. He planted over one million fruit trees of every variety: oranges, prunes, peaches, apples, lemons, plums, cherries, and even black walnuts. Woodson hired Bert Whitaker to manage the planting and care of the orchards. In 1893, they had a crew of 70 men and

60 horses working these orchards. Whitaker, a bachelor, was living in Mineral when I was growing up. I remember throwing rocks at his house one Halloween night and then hiding behind a tree as he shot a gun at us, or up in the air—I don't know which.

Woodson advertised extensively in farm and church magazines. Ultimately over $500,000 was spent promoting the land sales. He organized and promoted an exhibit of the Maywood Colony and Tehama County at the Chicago World's Fair in 1893. The Board of Supervisors of Tehama County appropriated $3,500 for this purpose. Woodson was very successful selling the lots and land to families who wished to come west. Eventually his land sales surrounded the town of Corning.

In 1893, the then partners developed 160 acres east of the railroad, known as the Maywood Addition. This new addition to the town of Corning included residential lots, a public park, and space for a cooperative cannery and packing house. Later, this area became the Maywood Packing Company, and today it is owned and operated by the Bell Carter Company. Two blocks east of the packing company, at 703 Walnut Street, was my grandparent's home, adjacent to what is now Woodson Park.

Woodson and Foster were involved in everything. They built the Maywood Hotel in 1899 on Main Street across from the Maywood Colony office as well as the railroad depot to accommodate the prospective colonists in grand style. The hotel was considered to be the last word in elegance with a ballroom on the second floor. It was three stories high with 43 rooms. The famous Palm Court brought the outdoors into the interior of the hotel. I remember going to dinner there with my parents and my grandmother when I was around the age of eight. I remember being wide-eyed, feeling elegant eating there. I own two wire benches that came from this famous Palm Court, given to me by Woodson's niece, Charlotte Reichle. After several fires, the land was sold and is now the location of the Corning City Hall. Woodson designed and built a new Maywood Colony Office in 1903. It was decorated

Maywood Hotel

in the old Spanish mission style with a red-tiled roof. It had a 70-foot observation tower with a wide balcony on top so that the prospective buyers could be taken up and impressed with the view of the town and the orchards. This tower is no longer there.

Olive trees were planted in the area; they grew better than other fruit trees in the soil around Corning because they were immune to the grasshoppers and jack rabbits that sometimes plagued the other fruit trees. The Mission variety was considered the best for the poorer soil and produced large olives. It is interesting to note that the olive trees planted in the rich river-bottom soil produced lots of small olives, while trees growing in the poorer soil had fewer but larger olives. At first olives were only used for oil until the arrival of the varieties Nevadillo Blanco and Manzanilla, which were cheaper to plant and grow.

Fred G. Beresford was born in Fremont, Nebraska, in 1865. His father was English, his mother Dutch. The family traveled by oxen team to California when he was one year old, so he learned to walk inside a covered wagon. The family arrived in Roseville, then moved to Oregon, and then back to Nebraska. Traveling was no problem for them, and I certainly inherited those travel genes from that side of my family. Beresford managed a large general store in Rock Springs, Wyoming, for the Sweetwater Coal Mining Company. There he met and married my grandmother, Nellie Victoria Kelsey, who had traveled from New York for her health.

Beresford was also a pioneer in the fruit and olive industry in Corning. He helped establish the Maywood Packing Company in 1904, which was owned by Warren Woodson. In 1905, a batch of olive saplings that were late in bearing was about to be discarded when my grandfather saved them. When the trees did produce, the olives were as big as plums. They were called Sevillano because they originated near Seville, Spain. Beresford then grafted this new olive to existing trees. The result was a big olive that became the queen of all olives, but it could only be grown successfully in the Corning area. He experimented until he discovered the right way to process this queen olive. The first pack was 16 tons. The yield gradually increased until it reached 6,000 tons a year. At one time, there were 11 olive processing and canning plants in Corning. The process developed by my grandfather is no longer used today, and the mammoth Sevillano olive is also gone. I remember when the company produced several different-sized olives; the "mammoth" was almost the size of a golf ball. The golf course at Rolling Hills Casino near Corning is named Sevillano Links after this famous olive from the past.

The Beresfords moved to Corning in 1897, certainly due to Woodson's promotions. When Fred died in 1922, he was the manager, secretary, and treasurer of the Maywood Packing Company (although he had no ownership in the company). At one time, he, with his brother Will, owned one of the largest producing prune orchards in the state. He was director of the California Prune Growers Association. I remember Uncle Will telling me that Fred told him to sell the prune orchard because the soil would not last. Will implied that he had not sold early enough. It seems to me that Will, who had been a jeweler in Amboy, Illinois, and followed his brother to Corning, was the financier and Fred Beresford the idea man. Will and his sister, Della, never lacked for money, while Fred's family never saved a dime. When Fred Beresford died in 1922, they owned their home and the one investment he had made with Woodson—the land and buildings in Mineral. Beresford died from an unknown illness at age 52; Nellie Victoria lived to be 87. I do not remember her ever being sick.

When Woodson and Beresford purchased Mineral in 1920, the recorded deed lists the legal description of the 480 acres plus the water and water ditches appurtenant to the land; what buildings were on the land I can only guess. The story I heard as I grew up was that Mineral was purchased as a summer place for olive workers, and both Woodson and Beresford were enthusiastic hunters and loved to fish. While the meadows had a large herd of black-tailed deer and 25 fish could easily be caught in a day, I do not believe that the purchase was made for those reasons. Woodson was a land developer, and Mineral offered cool temperatures to escape the brutal summers of the Sacramento Valley. Lassen Peak had been designated as a National Park in 1916, another possible incentive. The potential for future subdivisions and business was certainly there. The purchase price was reported to be $20,000. I have reason to believe this because, until my father died in 1962, the Elbert Hampton family had a note against the land for $20,000, and the business paid the interest yearly.

The purchase of Mineral was an equal partnership between Beresford and Woodson. Beresford died just two years later leaving his share to his wife and their son, my father, Husky (Harrold), who was attending the University of California in Berkeley to obtain a degree in chemistry. His dream of becoming a medical doctor vanished. There was no money, and he had his mother to support. He worked a short time for the Maywood Packing Company selling olives to the eastern market but quickly found this did not suit him. My parents were married in 1926; I was born in April of 1931. They already lived in Mineral then; why and how they made the decision to move to the mountains, I do not know. But I do know that neither one of them ever regretted living in Mineral. There was a contract with Woodson concerning the partnership for running the business of Mineral Camp Site.

In 1939, Woodson transferred his half of Mineral to my parents for an unknown sum. I remember that it had something to do with the mortgage on Uncle Will's garage for around $9,000. This was far below the value of Woodson's share. My parents always said that Woodson gave his half to them as payment for Fred's work with the Maywood Packing Company. And to a certain extent I am sure this was true, but I think that other factors also played into the decision. Woodson had only one son, Woody, who never worked a day in his life and never meant to. Woody and Grace, his wife, had no children and were too busy having fun to have any. My parents were doing all the work in Mineral, plus Mineral was probably not generating much income for Woodson. Add to this, my father did not like bookkeeping, so his reporting was probably not the best. There was an old letter in the safe pointing this out to him. As it turned out, I feel that I and my family, plus my brother and his family, reaped the benefits of Woodson's gift. We had a wonderful life growing up and living there for a good part of our lives in Mineral. ∞

Another view of the Woodson home in Mineral

HOTEL *Maywood* and LAND OFFICE of *Maywood Colony*
WARREN N. WOODSON
CORNING, CALIFORNIA

THE HEN THAT LAID THE CORNING EGG

4-13-'39.

Dear Harold:

           I am just in receipt of the financial report of our Mineral Campsite business for the year 1938.

           Mr. Miller writes that there is some question in his mind as to just how to dispose of the two items referred to in our partnership agreement, except by considering the items of $1721.38 and $2000. as having been contributed by you, regardless of the fact that one or both of this items, or a portion of them, may yet stand as an indebtednes of you personally, as an indebtedness of you and me jointly.

           Our business relations were so long unadjusted and consequently tangled that I thought these two items should in some way be covered in our first annual statement, but to avoid further confusion in this connection let this letter be as an agreement from and by me that our interests as of January first 1938 were equal regardless as to whether these two items still exist as your personal or our joint obligation.

           If Mr. Miller has written you as he has me his letter would tend do disconcert you and leave a question in your mind as to just how I understood the matter.

           While these two items are not dealt with in the financial report, and probably could not be, our partnership agreement shows that we started on an equal financial basis on January Lst. 1938.

           Attach this letter to your copy of our partnership agreement for further evidence should any question arise in the future relative to our interests in the Mineral Campsite proposition.

                                      Yours very truly,

                                      W N Woodson

Katie and Husky Beresford

CHAPTER 4

MY FAMILY

I was born in Red Bluff, California, in April of 1931, that being the closest hospital and doctor to Mineral at that time. The distance was 43 miles over a paved mountain road. My parents had moved to Mineral after their marriage. Their first home was a small cabin of two bedrooms located behind the Hampton store.

The small cabin my parents called home was next to the Fripp house. Warren Woodson's sister was Mrs. Fripp who probably built her cabin sometime after 1920. Our cabin was one of a few cabins scattered around the property not in a subdivision or on deeded land. The cabin owners were relatives, friends, or special employees. Over the years, most of these cabins fell down or were torn down, as was the case with the Fripp cabin. However, there is one cabin remaining from that time located at 38123 Conard Avenue in the Meadow View Subdivision developed in 1950 by my father who incorporated this house into the plans (the various subdivisions that were developed are discussed later in Chapter 13). Woodson and his family used the Hamptons' home, which had been the first hotel, for their summer use.

My father, Husky, was only called his given name, Harrold, by his mother. Everyone else, from guests to employees, called him

Cabin at 38123 Conard Avenue, Mineral, c. 1920s

"Husky." This was not a very suitable name as he was not a large man as the name implies. He was slightly over six feet tall and would be considered skinny even in his elder years. He acquired his nickname in high school as a basketball star on the Corning team. His slight build had somehow inspired this odd name. He and his best friend, Curtiss Wetter, who later became the Superior Judge in Tehama County, went to the University of California in Berkeley to further their education. He earned a letter in basketball at Berkeley.

Husky Beresford

You have to know that six foot one was tall in those days. He and Curtiss joined the Army Air Corp during World War I, only to be stricken with the endemic flu that killed thousands of people worldwide. Husky told me that he spent his entire enlistment period in the Corps in bed, flat on his back, with men dying all around him. Judge Wetter told me that my father had saved his life in the hospital as they both lay ill with this terrible flu. How he did that, I am not sure.

Husky's interest in medicine was a great benefit for me as I grew up. I was always falling and skinning my knees or something of that sort, and my father was always there to put the methylate on. He never used cotton to apply this liquid, he just poured it on, and it ran down my skinny legs. I can still see the methylate—a popular, bright orange liquid disinfectant—and the dirt decorating my leg for the remainder of the day.

Husky was born in 1898 and spent most of his adult years in Mineral owning and operating Mineral Lodge. He was extremely happy with this independent life even if it meant long hours—seven days a week with little time off. He was not the slap-on-the-back, great greeter type of person you might envision as the proprietor of a mountain resort. He was, however, a great listener; he seemed to always be on the front porch of the lodge either walking or sitting, which meant he was usually available to talk to any and all guests who arrived. He was a mentor to all of his employees and treated them all as if they were a member of the family. I think he truly felt that if they were in his employment they were more than "help."

I was in my teens before I realized that people were in business to make money. My father felt that we, and that included his family, were there to please the customer, and believe you me, we all went out of our way to accomplish this. If our motel units were full on a busy night in the summer months, Husky would call all the next resorts along Hwy 36 to find rooms for the people he could not accommodate. Usually these people stayed for dinner, and they usually came back another year. If a hitchhiker was still standing by the road after dark, my father fed him dinner, put him in a motel unit for the night, and fed him breakfast the next morning before sending him on his way. One, Joe Dubeck, stayed and worked for us one winter, and I am sure he would have stayed longer if the housekeeper, Helen, had not tried to end his free life with marriage!

My father was a great sportsman. He played golf, loved to fly fish and to hunt quail, ducks, pheasants, and black-tailed deer. He had grown up shooting birds on the Sacramento River and was an excellent shot, using a 28-gauge shotgun for hunting. Husky was not, however, a good businessman because he simply did not value money. My mother told me that when they first came to Mineral, he would put money just any old place, like the V's formed by the two-by-fours in the unfinished interior of the office. She would gather up all the money and keep it until he needed it. I believe he was successful at Mineral Lodge because he took such good care of the customers, and he had well-kept facilities. The rich and the not-

Husky Beresford and Ross Parker back from hunting in Turner Mountain

so-rich came by our door, and we were to treat them all the same, from the night watchman at Diamond International in Red Bluff to the president of Standard Oil from San Francisco, and everyone in-between. All were valued customers.

Husky was a wonderful father to me. I will always remember how understanding he was when I clashed with my mother as a pre-teenager. We had a live-in housekeeper from the time I was eight until she left when I was twelve. Apparently I did not have to help around house when she was there, and then suddenly I was expected to help with the housework and, at least, pick up my own clothes. This caused a great deal of conflict between my mother and me. I would often run upstairs crying, and my father would come up, talk to me, and calm me down. I do not believe that he ever did much to solve the problem as this was not his style. He let things resolve themselves; I never saw him hit a situation head on, he just waited. I am not sure if he was that smart, or he just hated conflict.

I will always remember when I was 18 and ready to enter college. Mineral Lodge had burned down, and the insurance adjuster was there to settle the matter. Because he was staying at the Lodge, my parents took him to Chester for dinner, and I went along. We were at the Bear Club that had a bar, dinner, and dancing. I was dancing with my father when he said to me, "Jo Ann, smart women don't drink too much. Look around and see how some women are acting, then look at your mother. She never drinks too much." This was good advice. I occasionally did not follow it, but I never forgot it.

Husky taught me to dance, a feat I never would have accomplished without his constant tutelage as I was totally left-footed. The best thing he did for me was make sure that I attended the University of California at Berkeley. I had some idea that San Jose State was for me, but when we talked about college, only "Cal" was discussed, so off I went to Berkeley in the fall of 1949. I was never sorry. He told me later that I was a fine country girl, but I needed a little polish, and he was right. I am comfortable with people from all walks of life due to my growing up in Mineral and at the University.

Husky died at the early age of 67 from prostate cancer. He rarely touched a vegetable; meat and potatoes were his fare. He could choose this because we always ate in the restaurant or "Coffee Shop." He was sincerely missed by all his friends and guests who frequented Mineral, but more so by his daughter.

My mother was named Catherine Amanda after two of her aunts. After she married my father, she added the name Beresford, which gave her a name she felt was much too long for a signature. She did not want to burden me with such, so I was named Joan with no middle name. This was no problem for me except when I was a flight attendant for United Airlines since they required a middle initial. If you did not have one you used X. So Joan X it was. She meant my name to be Jo Ann, a name I have since taken as my own. My mother, like my father, was never addressed by either of her given names. She was Katie to her family and everyone else.

Katie was born in 1899 in Dixon, California, a small farming community west of Sacramento. She was one of eight children, six boys and two girls. Both of her parents were of German descent who came from the same small town of Javenstedt in northern Germany near the Danish border. In fact, most of the early

Catherine "Katie" Beresford, JoAnn's mother

population of Dixon came from this German town and all were related. Her father, Jacob, came to the United States at twelve with two younger brothers to live with an aunt and uncle. Her mother was born in Dixon and spoke German; however, German was not spoken in her home, only English. So my mother only understood a few words of that language.

Jacob was a harsh father. My mother never had a nice word to say about him, and no tears were shed at his funeral. He died long before I was born, and I have thought a lot about him because there is not a mean or unpleasant trait in any of his descendants. My conclusion is that he must have been a very unhappy man and took his frustrations out on his family.

Lena Rohwer, my mother's mother, was just the opposite. They all loved her; she was the backbone of the family. She lived to age 94 and farmed her land with an iron fist. Her sacks of barley and wheat had to be full, no shrinkage for her. She sent five of her children to the University in Berkeley, including my mother, using her chicken and egg money. She always had a large barnyard full of chickens; it was a real adventure for me as a mountain girl to hunt the eggs when we visited her.

My mother told me that when Lena first married Jacob, she went into town with her horse and buggy and was told she should not be there because she belonged on the ranch. The story is that either Jacob or his brother, Chris, shot her horse right there. As I grew up visiting her over the years, I became aware that she did not leave her house and had not for several years.

My mother was a star basketball player in high school, reigned as May Queen for the Dixon May Fair, and earned a B.A. from the University of California, Berkeley. She taught English and history in Corning High School where they dedicated the yearbook to her in 1926. She was the postmistress in Mineral for over 35 years and was charming and well liked. Unfortunately, due to her father's harshness, she never had the confidence in herself that she deserved.

She met Husky in Corning where she had come to teach. Katie was hired because of her religion. There were a lot of churches in Corning, and they had to spread the teachers around evenly. She was young, danced with the high school students, played bridge, and was denounced by her minister for these behaviors. Interestingly, religion was never discussed in our home. Neither my brother nor I were baptized, and my mother only attended church for weddings and funerals. Richfield, three miles north of Corning, had a dance hall at that time. My mother was not allowed by the school board to attend these dances, so she sat with my father in his car and watched.

As I grew up, many of my mother's former students came to Mineral, and, as the years went by, they started looking much older than my mother as she never did look her age. When she died at age 89, she did not look a day over 75.

My father was postmaster when they first came to Mineral but gave the job to my mother after a year. He did not like to sit still, but someone in the family needed to do the job. It worked out well for both of them, as she could do the bookkeeping for the business along with the job at the Post Office. It also gave her an independent income apart from the Mineral Lodge.

The Post Office was open six days a week, but she also had to process the mail on Sundays for several years. She retired with a nice pension that she always felt she had earned. But she lived in constant fear that the postal inspector would come unexpectedly any time. She was never late to open the Post Office at 8:00 a.m. even in the dead of winter in a blizzard and never closed early either. She only relaxed for the two weeks following the inspector's visit. The government did get their money's worth from her.

Mineral Lodge had the only telephone in Mineral, so along with the Post Office, my mother had to handle the telephone as well for many years. This meant placing calls for people, taking all incoming

Postcard of unknown cabin showing Mineral postmark from 1910 (courtesy Tina Jones)

calls for anyone in the vicinity of Mineral and seeing that the messages got delivered.

My mother hated the telephone company because she did not get paid anything by the company for her time and trouble. When the telephone company wanted to build a facility in Mineral in order to expand the service, my mother would not sign the deed for the land they wanted to buy. My father somehow tricked her into signing, and she never forgot this either. She had an elephant memory for any slight she had suffered, and this clouded her life some.

After her retirement from the Post Office and my father's death, she moved to Red Bluff where she enjoyed playing bridge with her many friends. She came to Mineral every summer for several years after her move to count the money for the Lodge and help us any other way that she could. She had an amazing amount of energy.

My parents loved to play cards. My mother played bridge whenever she could, and they both played cut-throat pinochle (three handed) with a vengeance. They spent many evenings at home in the winter months playing cribbage. It seemed that my father won more than Katie did. I can still hear her saying "Damn you, Husky, you won again." Despite the fact that she did not like losing a card game to Husky, they had a good relationship and marriage. They both worked long hours but enjoyed time away from the business together. In the summer months, they would go fishing with only bread and butter, cooking and eating the fish my father caught out in the open. Katie did not fish, but she loved being outdoors. In the fall they spent many hours in the woods picking up tree branches left from logging to bring home to cut up for their winter wood. Their "garage" was a good 50' x 30' in size, and my mother felt secure only when it was full of cut wood for the winter. They went four or five times a year to San Francisco for a night in the city and Berkeley to see a California Bears football game.

Katie was not an easy mother in some respects because she was very critical, and I could rarely ever please her. In retrospect, I feel that her father, Jacob, was behind this. Fortunately I was able to spend time with Dr. Thatcher, a psychiatrist, who helped me work through this, and Katie and I ended up good friends. As a mother she was always there when I needed her. She made sure I was well dressed for every function I ever attended. She always listened to my complaints and troubles, except when it involved a teacher, and then she would not listen to any of it. She taught me the difference between right and wrong. You always did it the right way in her book. The only thing she ever did, which was somewhat against the rules, was to ask the ration board during World War II for permission to buy a bicycle. She said she needed it to deliver special-delivery letters. The bicycle was really for me at age 12. This was truly the only way I could have had a bicycle. To my knowledge, no letter was ever delivered with it.

Katie was a great influence on her grandchildren whom she kept sometimes when they attended high school in Red Bluff. They knew she only did something the right way, and they still talk about her. She was always going to give someone "the dickens." She never did of course, and they always laughed about it and are still wondering what "the dickens" was. My nephew lived with her for two winters when he was over 20. She told me that he refused to turn off the water to her plants in the front of the house when she asked him to. I asked her what she did, wondering how you can discipline a 20 year old. She said, "I did not talk to him for two days." He did everything she asked after that.

She paid her bills the day they arrived and cleaned the house the day before the housekeeper came. She was charming to everyone she ever met. I consider her the "Grande Dame" in my life.

My brother, Fred, was born three years after me almost to the day, my birthday being April 13 and his April 11. I do not remember being jealous of his arrival, although my mother told me I told her to put him down and hold me. I was bossy at age three. Fred was very shy as a young child, even though we grew up around a lot of people. Relatives who came to visit were his worst fear. He would run to the top of the hill next to the Lodge and hide out around the

Fred Beresford with his Christmas trees

water tanks as long as he could. He did not like the extra attention meted out by these people.

Fred inherited a German temper from our mother and was easily angered. I felt that no one should have such a temper and thought that I could stop his behavior by constantly teasing and annoying him. He would fly at me with his fists swinging, and I had to run for help, but I never stopped badgering him. He carried this temper with him his entire life; however, it was never directed at people, although the Giants baseball team and a malfunctioning vehicle received direct hits. He broke furniture and other items if the Giants had a bad day. One day when he was harvesting Christmas trees and his Power Wagon had broken down for the third time that day, he jumped out of the truck and started yelling and throwing rocks at the Power Wagon. The young boys working for him ran from the scene and hid behind trees they were so frightened by his behavior. They had never seen this side of his personality before as he usually had a smile on his face and appeared to be easygoing.

Fred loved baseball and hillbilly music; growing up he would spend hours batting a rock with a baseball bat and listening to his music. I ended up liking the music but not the baseball. He also attended the University of California in Berkeley, playing on the baseball team there. He did not find his true profession until after graduation. He should have majored in forestry, because he fell in love with growing Christmas trees and spent the rest of his life cultivating and harvesting these trees, which he sold to the wholesale market. He and his wife, Sue, along with my husband, George, and I invested in land near Paynes Creek for a tree farm. Fred worked on the tree farm and we ran Mineral Lodge. The trees were to be our retirement. It did not work out quite this way, and the land is now George's "Choose and Cut Christmas Tree Farm."

Back Row (left to right): Sue Beresford, Katie Beresford, Husky Beresford, Jo Ann Perkins. Front Row (left to right)): Heidi Perkins, George Perkins, Michael Beresford, Fred Beresford, c. 1960.

Fred later had two Christmas trees farms in Oregon and three in the Sacramento Valley in California. Not one of these farms survives today due to the changing wholesale tree business and Fred's inability to manage costs easily. He had a talent for growing beautiful trees. He learned how to shape the trees as they grew and what methods worked best for survival of the thousands of seedlings he planted every year. He dearly loved his work in the field. He arose most mornings around 4:00 a.m. and worked hard until late into the afternoon.

Fred was a little over six feet tall, strong, and extremely good looking. He could do the Russian dance with his knees bent, arms folded, putting one leg out a time, and he could swing from the rafters in the Rafter Room in the Mineral Bar—both extremely difficult maneuvers. He was easy going, and everyone liked to be around him, but he really preferred to be by himself. That's why he liked working outside with his trees.

As I have mentioned, he loved the Giants baseball team. One time he decided to take his boys to San Francisco to see a game. He kept telling David, age 6, that he was going to see the Giants. David came home quite disappointed; he had expected to see real, people giants, not a baseball game. One time when his boys were small, teenagers from out of town were speeding down Fred's street as he was getting ready to step into the shower. He grabbed a baseball bat and came out swinging with only a towel on, threatening the speeders. They never returned! He never liked to ski as much as I did, although he knew how. Every once in a while he would put on a pair of skis just to see if he could still do it.

Fred dearly loved his bacon and eggs with butter piled high on the toast, and he ate this every morning, ignoring the latest heath findings. He was not happy without his meat and potatoes and his high-fat breakfasts. He thought he had inherited his mother's long lifespan; he felt that his hard, physical work kept him immune from harm. He ignored his doctor's warning that he had a bad heart and, instead, changed doctors. Unfortunately for him, and for me, his lifestyle caught up with him, and he died quickly of a heart attack at the early age of 63. Far too young!

I graduated from Berkeley in 1953 with a major in Social Welfare; I was not interested in any job in an office in a large city because I was looking for adventure in the world. I was lucky to be hired by United Airlines as, what was then called, a stewardess. After six weeks of training in Cheyenne, Wyoming, I was stationed in Denver, Colorado. This was a great place for me, close to the mountains and skiing. I met George Perkins there, and we were married in 1955. George grew up in Chicago and had graduated with a business major from the University of Colorado. After six months in Colorado Springs, we returned to Mineral to live. Fred married Sue Sartain from Colusa in the summer of 1956, and they also came to Mineral to live. My father had obtained a lease from the Lassen Park Company to operate the ski area in Lassen Park for the winter months. Mineral Lodge needed the winter business, and my father needed the family to help manage the Lodge and ski area.

We spent the next 20 years in Mineral raising our families, operating the businesses, and enjoying life. We all worked many long hours in sometimes difficult circumstances, but we all got along, and we never had a major problem, which is pretty amazing when you consider six individuals and seven diverse businesses. I believe the major reason that it worked so well was because of my father's attitude, and the fact that we all had good marriages.

We lived in separate houses but ate either together or separately in the Coffee Shop. Husky did not believe in expressing an opinion as to how you should live your life, and he kept my mother from expressing hers. I am sure there were times that they did not approve of our actions, but we never heard about it.

Each person had a special responsibility but also was obligated to help out in any of the different parts of the business. George had the ski area, bar, and bookkeeping; Fred had the grocery store; I had the Coffee Shop, Gift Shop, and the ski area food service. Husky had the cabins and motels units; Sue did whatever was asked of her and especially helped me out much of the time; Katie still had the Post Office and money counting.

Sue was truly amazing. She was very pretty and looked a lot like Jacqueline Kennedy. She had graduated from the Katherine Branson private school in Marin County and had never worked a day in her life. The adjustment to Mineral must have been a shock to her because we all worked most of the time. But she never, ever complained and was always willing to do whatever was asked of her. We were very good friends and shared many good times in and out of Mineral. We especially enjoyed our trips to San Francisco every spring to purchase merchandise for the Gift Shop.

My oldest child, Heidi Ann, was born in 1957, followed by Fred and Sue's sons, Michael Kelsey in 1959 and David Mitchell in 1960. George and I had two more daughters, Lynn Christine in 1961 and Jody Catherine in 1962. We also took in Nils Johnson as a foster son in 1965. So we had two nice families that we blended together quite a bit of the time. I helped raise my two nephews, and Sue was part-time mother for my girls and Nils.

In the summer months, we worked all day, every day, so for those three months we hired a college girl for each family. This worked very well and freed us from our major childcare responsibilities. The children had the swimming pool for chief entertainment, and our baby-sitters were good for hiking and other fun. One summer they all hiked over 99 miles climbing mountains and other trails in and out of the Park. We also put the children to work, starting with small jobs at Mineral Lodge. They could all run a cash register and count change by the age of six or seven. Our children all attended and graduated from the elementary school in Mineral. They all learned to ski at an early age and are still spectacular skiers.

We suffered a great tragedy when Michael Kelsey was killed at age 17 on his motorcycle. Michael was a great skier, one of the first to do aerials while jumping on skis. He loved motorcycles and was a bit of daredevil. He believed he was invincible, yet we lost him. A great sadness for us all. ℰ◌

MY MOTHER'S WEDDING

I was working in Denver, Colorado, for United Air Lines as a stewardess when George Perkins asked me to marry him. This was in April of 1955, and the wedding was scheduled for September 10th. My mother demanded that I come home in June to prepare for the event. I had some trouble with this summons. Why was it going to take so much time, and what was I going to do about it? I thought all I had to do was purchase the wedding dress. I had never spent any time thinking about my wedding because I always thought I would be an old maid with a cat farm. I was unaware that my mother had been thinking about it for years.

I came home at the end of June and actually didn't do much about the wedding because my mother was in high gear on the subject. I spent a lot of my time on Battle Creek at the local swimming hole. In fairness to my mother, she did have a lot to do to prepare for the event. Because we owned Mineral Lodge, the reception would naturally be there. We had the cooks and plenty of help for this, but Mineral had no church, so there was no place for the ceremony, except our front yard. The yard was big enough and mostly lawn, but it was not as fancy as my mother would have liked. It was hard to have flowers in Mineral because of the black-tailed deer that loved to eat anything. My mother had cages built of chicken wire that she put over her flower beds every night to keep the deer from destroying everything. She had this problem licked, but the even bigger one was the land behind the house. It had been used to store auto wrecks from the Mineral Lodge garage for several years. My father had promised her that these unsightly vehicles would be removed by the time of the wedding.

Well, the summer went on, and the vehicles did not move. To add insult to injury, a few more of the same were added to this menagerie. My mother almost killed the poor tow truck driver who delivered the latest items. My father, bless his soul, kept assuring her that the wrecks would be gone by September 10th. I am not sure what his plan was, but by the first of September, all of the vehicles were still there, including the newest arrivals. As you can imagine, my mother was quite upset. She could not physically remove the unsightly items herself, so what could she do? Bill Bruener, a close friend, came up with the solution. He put up two strands of rope then leaned cut Christmas trees against the ropes to screen off the offending items. This took some 50 trees from our own land. The cars could hardly be seen and peace was restored. I am sure that most of the guests never realized what was behind the trees.

Then there were the flowers for decoration of the Lodge and reception area. Mrs. McQueen, who lived in the little, fairy house on Scenic Avenue, spent all summer making imitation carnations out of Kleenex tissues. At the time, I did not see anything unusual about this; sometimes I even helped to make them and delivered all the Kleenex to her. I am sure the guests were not aware of these fake carnations either because they were backed by fresh evergreens from the forest.

George, the groom, was not planning on any wedding guests. He came from Chicago, his parents had retired to the Virgin Islands, and his one brother was overseas in the Air Force. Unannounced, the day before the wedding, his cute blonde cousin, Barbara Musler, arrived from Sacramento. My uncles said he was there in quality, not quantity. So it was a great wedding. All my relatives and friends from everywhere were there. The cake was the biggest cake the Red Bluff Bakery had ever made, and my mother could relax. She didn't have to do it again, because I was the only daughter!

Barbara Musler and her husband, Jay, retired to Mineral several years later. There is a plaque on the Mineral Lodge porch in Jay's memory. He piloted B-24 planes in World War II.

CHAPTER 5

Growing Up in Mineral

Mineral was a great place to be as a child. It was a small area with few children, but there was always someone to play with; you were never lonely or bored. You were not confined to your age bracket. If you were age five, you played with maybe someone age ten or age four, it simply did not matter. It was like any port in a storm—you were tolerated or you welcomed the company. You were included in most adult activities as well; life was very interesting from this standpoint because you never felt left out. Bullying, as we know it today, was not tolerated by the children or the adults.

I took a cultural anthropology class from Shasta College a few years ago. One of the members of the class was a local American Indian who explained why his people had such a hard time leaving the reservation. The reservation gave them such a sense of security that the outside world did not provide; therefore, members of the tribe were not comfortable living anyplace else. Mineral was like living on a reservation because of the strong support system it provided.

The population of Mineral consisted mostly of families who were employees of the National Park Service that administered Lassen Volcanic Park, the U. S. Forest Service, or the California State

Division of Highways. These families lived in their respective compounds where housing was provided for them. The balance of the population worked for either the Mineral Mill or the Mineral Lodge and lived in the Cool Air subdivision across from the Lodge. The Mineral School had 14-18 students when I started in the first grade and the same number of students when I graduated from the eighth grade. Social life centered on the school, the Mineral Lodge, and the Park Service Recreation Hall. Everyone was invited and welcomed to all the events. We learned first aid and occasionally were able to see a movie in the Park Rec Hall. Potlucks and school events were held in the school building; dancing and other social activities took place at the Mineral Lodge or the Rec Hall.

Everybody knew everybody. I never addressed an older person as Mr. or Mrs. I used their first names, from the mechanic at the mill to the superintendent of the Park Service. You were welcomed in any of your classmates' homes, and they were certainly welcomed into yours without an invitation. A skinned knee was doctored by the nearest adult, and by the same token, discipline was handed out to whoever needed it by whomever was on hand. You never felt alone in the world; there was always someone nearby to give whatever support or encouragement was needed. There were no secrets in Mineral; everybody knew all of your activities, your good features, and your bad ones. Privacy was traded for respect and support.

As I remember, we did not have many toys to play with, but there was the whole world to play in. We made pretend houses between logs, we waded in streams with our bare feet, and we climbed trees and made trees houses. We seemed to have great imaginations when it came to occupying our spare time. In the winter, we built snow igloos and snow angels, had snowball fights, skied, and slid off roofs for the most fun. There were horses and cows to watch, and we also worried about the mother cats with kittens.

There was a female, long-haired, yellow cat named Fiffe who was tame but did not seem to have a home. She lived among the many cabins on the Lodge property. One time my friend Rosemary's mother, Nell, told us we could bring Fiffe and her kittens to her house. When we went to get the cat and five kittens, we discovered five more kittens in another part of the building. We felt the extra five had been abandoned so took them home to Nell's along with Fiffe and her five. The cat never flinched and raised all 10 kittens. Nell was amazed that Fiffe had 10 kittens and told everyone about it. Rosemary and I never said a word, but we have had good laughs about it over the years.

There was always a pet deer around. They had been found abandoned as fawns and raised by local people. These people thought they were doing nature a favor, but probably not, because as these fawns grew up they became problems. They did not know where they belonged and roamed the neighborhood looking for a place to fit in. They were dangerous because they used their front hoofs to strike at you. I remember climbing a rail fence with a deer right behind me with its hoofs trying to reach me. Another time, when it was almost dark, I could not get to my house because a deer was between me and home.

Nature was right out our door, and we took advantage of it. We collected polliwog eggs in the spring and watched them hatch. I was scared of frogs, but loved getting the eggs. Once they hatched, I returned them to the pond I got them from. I felt I was helping out the frogs. We collected wild flowers and pressed them for an unknown future use. It was an exciting time and place to grow up.

Most people are lucky to have two adult parents to raise them. But by growing up at Mineral Lodge, my brother, Fred, and I were fortunate to have additional people around to assist our parents. Employees and guests took great interest in us; both of our parents were always there, and we grew up under constant vigilance and discipline if necessary. Until I was eight years old, we lived in an apartment above the Lodge. There were nine hotel rooms and three employee rooms upstairs as well. We all ate in the Lodge restaurant. It was, in some respects, one big happy family. Two waitresses who lived in the employee rooms had daughters a few years older than I. I remember staying the night with either one of them quite often. They were always putting my hair up in those hard metal curlers before we went to bed. If my hair did not turn out to their satisfaction, they just combed out the curls in the morning. I did not like this because the curlers were uncomfortable to sleep on, but I never complained.

Fred was three years younger than I and easier to raise because he would play for hours in a sandbox behind the Lodge. I was always underfoot asking questions and would not stay in one place very long. Fred told me later that he hated staying in the sandbox, but he did it. He was encouraged by the guests and employees to imitate

Fred Beresford (age 5) and Jo Ann Beresford (age 8)

Joe Lewis, the famous boxer. Fred thought it was great fun and went around socking people until his actions became a problem. My parents had a hard time breaking him of this bad habit.

Mineral had a Girl Scout troop. Emma Potts was the leader with Thelma Rex as her assistant. I look back on my time in the Scouts with fond memories because I learned so much. They taught me how to make a bed properly, how to set a table with the silverware in the right places, and how to identify the local fauna and flora. I can still identify most evergreens and all the local wildflowers. We had high adventure on our first camp out. The leaders decided to camp off the Viola Road, a dirt road that connected Highway 36 with Viola, because it was close to home. When the leaders were checking out the area a few days before the event, they ran into a big black bear. We still camped there, but we did not sleep much because we were constantly waking up to see if a bear was near. The leaders strung a rope between two trees, and we all tied our sleeping bag covers to it. I guess the idea was to deter the bear with this line of beige material.

We never saw a bear that year, but a few years later, several black bears showed up at our local dump. The dump was just a large trench where we tossed garbage—easy pickings for the bears. The locals thought that these bears were transplants from Yosemite because the bears were too pesky and familiar with people. It was also hoped that the bears would revert back to their natural habitat, which I believe did happen. Over the years we would have an influx of bears at the dump, the population would decrease, and then another group would show up. The bears that arrived in the later years were much bolder and more accustomed to humans. Several people were surprised to see a bear looking in their window. One small bear even entered my ex-husband's kitchen when he left the door open to get his camera from his car. He had to throw hot water on the bear to make it leave. Bears were good entertainment after dark at the dump—you could sit in the car and watch them for as long as you wanted. The dump was the place to go during my teens and later. Now the dump has no open garbage, so the bears are discouraged from hanging around. Sadly, this form of entertainment is gone, probably never to return.

The only bear I ever saw away from the dump is an experience I am glad only happened once. I was hiking to Black Rock with my friend Minki and her two daughters. We were two or three miles below the Hole-in-the-Ground campground. Minki was ahead of us around a bend in the trail when we saw this large black bear walking toward the trail we were on. He stopped with his enormous paws over a small downed tree, looked at us, we looked at him—and he ran in the opposite direction. My father had always told me a bear would run from you if you met it in the woods, and he was right. I can still see those large black paws with their long nails over that log and recall the longest moment of my life.

Weather dominated our lives in Mineral. It was a main source of excitement and drama. You never knew quite what to expect—it might snow for a day, then rain and melt all the snow off; or it might rain two days, then snow two feet or more. The wind blew at either gale force or as a gentle breeze. We never knew if the electricity would be on. If it went out, it might be two days before it was restored. PG&E never informed us what to expect. Mineral's elevation of 4,900 feet seemed to be a dividing line between rain and snow. If a storm came straight from Alaska, it snowed; if the storm dipped south before coming ashore, it rained. Wind was a major source of concern because of the tall trees, especially the pine trees with their shallow roots. A strong wind accompanied by inches of rain could and would blow down trees, roots and all.

Morgan Summit, elevation 5,700, five miles east on Highway 36, was a constant source of problems in heavy weather. The highway sign mandating chains on a car's rear tires was located across from Mineral Lodge. People often did not have chains or did not have the money to purchase them, and they were afraid to continue on in bad weather. Real problems developed if the highway eastbound closed because the plows could not keep up. Many times it rained for days and the culverts under the highway plugged up, causing

Sue and Fred Beresford

flooding, again stopping traffic. The Mineral Store was the hub of all activity in stormy weather, and, as children, we were always hanging around to catch the latest: How much snow on the summit? How many cars were off the road? Where did the tree blow down? To a child of the city, I guess this does not sound very interesting, but to us, it was the spice of our lives.

The record snowfall in 1937, with over 12 feet in a series of storms, had people walking by our second-story windows. One terrible storm in the 1960s pulled in a Pacific typhoon with frightful wind and rain for days. The wind blew so hard it lifted the front porch of the Lodge up, and all the posts fell down. Many trees were uprooted at their base, one going through a cabin. The second year we operated the Lassen Park Ski Area, major storms in late March of 1958 put down over 27 feet of snow, and we had to close the area. It was impossible to keep a trench open for the surface lift to operate. My brother, Fred, could tell you the dates of the biggest storms we had over the years. I really miss stormy weather.

My birth year of 1931 was during the Great Depression that began in 1929. My family never talked about the Depression. Times were not easy and money was not plentiful, but neither of my parents complained or discussed the situation. I grew up not knowing until I was much older that I was a Depression baby. There were no large families then; my friends were either only children or had one sibling. My family, being in business, must certainly have felt the pinch, but money was never mentioned. I was never told I could not have something because of money, or that I could not go someplace because we could not afford it. Mineral was a simple place to live; there was not much that took money, so maybe that was the reason. I was taught to turn off lights not in use, I received hand-me-down clothing from older children, and my outgrown dresses went to younger children. It was the accepted thing to do.

There were many homeless men roaming the country at that time. They were called tramps or hobos. Not many came through Mineral, but when they did, everyone paid attention and watched them. They were, for the most part, harmless; they just went from town to town looking for work. If they found no work, they knocked on a door and asked for something to eat. Living in the original Hampton homestead which faced Hwy 36, we had no neighbors, but we did have a party-line telephone (our ring was five longs). I remember men coming to the door asking for food. My mother was very afraid of them and called my father to come as quickly as he could. The first time he arrived with a shotgun because my mother was so frightened. After that he just came to calm my mother while she fed the man.

I remember people coming in the store asking how far it was to the next town, saying they did not know if they had enough gas, food, or money to go much further. I do not remember anybody helping them, but I worried about them for days afterward. Car caravans of gypsies came through Mineral often. The women wore long colorful skirts, great dangle earrings, and long strands of beads. It was high alert when they arrived; it was thought they would steal items and hide them in their skirts, which I am sure they did.

The spring and fall were interesting times for us as cattle and sheep were driven through Mineral from the valley to their summer pastures. There were herds of different sizes. The largest band of cattle was owned by McKenzie and Stover. It took over an hour before the last cow disappeared up the road. We did not get in the way of the cattle or sheep; we watched from behind fences or from the Mineral Lodge porch as the scene unfolded. It was such fun to see the cowboys and sheepherders with their dogs keeping the animals moving. They always had a mule or a donkey with bell around its neck at the end of the drive.

My great adventure with sheep occurred when I was eight. My mother had purchased a new dress for me in Red Bluff. I woke hearing the sheep baaing, jumped out of bed, put on my new dress, and ran out the door, following the sheep. Where they were going I don't know. But I followed behind them until I was above the Forest Service station, which is about a mile. Then I heard a horn honking, and my father telling me to get in the car. I wonder to this day how far I would have gone if my father had not found me. I don't remember any punishment for my actions, but I never followed another herd anyplace ever again.

It was fortunate that I grew up in Mineral, as I never would have learned to dance otherwise. We had community dances almost every Saturday night during the winter months. The Lodge had a great room for this purpose. It was separated from the bar proper by restrooms and a back bar. It had access to liquid refreshments but was separated from those who only chose to drink. I do not remember any falling-down drunks, but I am sure most people imbibed some. Most everyone came to these dances, and everyone was welcomed. The best part was that everyone had a good time. The dances started around 7:00 or 8:00 in the evening and were over by midnight. Most of the music was provided by the piano. Emma Potts, whose husband was a park ranger, did most of the playing with my mother filling in. There was a jukebox in the back bar, and this was used with the volume turned up when the piano player needed a rest.

I would have missed many good times if it were not for these dances as I was very shy and self-conscious. Most of the music was ballroom, but we also danced the polka and the schottische. Men were not fussy who they danced with—they just wanted to dance. I did not dare refuse them because that would have been impolite. I just did the best I could, which probably was not very good, but I did sort of get the hang of it after awhile. You did not have to worry about what your partner thought about your dancing—they simply did not care. No one was a wallflower; you just jumped up and down as best you could. This is where my father stepped in. He taught me how to follow him smoothly. I can still hear him say, "easy, easy, just glide along." My learning to dance did not happen overnight—it took years. Luckily by the time I was in high school, my dancing skills were passable, and I no longer worried about it. Due to these dances and my father's diligence, I have enjoyed a lifetime of dancing.

*Jo Ann's first home. She lived here during the summers
until she was 5 or 6 years old.*

Hampton's (left) and garage (right) looking east along Hwy 36E, c. 1915

CHAPTER 6

THE MINERAL LODGES

Paramount to any discussion about Mineral is the Mineral Lodge. The resort was not only the source of income for my family; it was the focus of our life. The resort business is not easy because it is, and was, a 24/7, 365 day commitment, compounded by weather. Anything and everything we did revolved around the management and ownership of the Lodge. It was not only my immediate family's chief interest, but also the most important element in the lives of our employees and other members of the community. It was, and is, the heart of the social life in Mineral.

From the 1890s to present day, five different complexes represent the resort per se, the first being the Bert Hampton home that served as a hotel for travelers, whether in the hay loft of the barn or upstairs in the house itself. As travel over the Tehama County Wagon Road (now State Highway 36) increased, Hampton constructed two more buildings farther west—one to serve food, called the Cook Shack, and a second as a store of general merchandise. These were built on the level land just west of the present-day Lodge. For those who have been around for a while, the Cook Shack was located where the swimming pool was from 1955 to 1995. For overnight accommodations, Hampton built cabins just east and north of his store. These cabins had a woodstove for cooking and heating and no inside plumbing; water

Mineral Camp Site

View of two-story grocery store and garage (photograph by H.C. Linn)
(John Nopel/CSU Chico Special Collections)

came from a ditch and was carried by the renter. The cabins were not large, consisting of not more than 300-400 square feet. These accommodations, which seem rustic by our standards today, were considered ample for the time and place of the early 1900s. Some of these cabins are still standing today.

After my grandfather and Woodson purchased the property in 1920, they replaced Hampton's store with a two-story retail building with living quarters upstairs. They changed the name to Mineral Camp Site, modernized the existing cabins, built additional cabins, and added tent platforms for campers. A garage and gas station was constructed across the wagon road for the new mode of transportation, the automobile. They replaced the ditches that furnished water with a piped distribution system serviced by a spring and a water tank high on the hill west of the complex. A generator was installed behind the gas station to provide electric power. The water and power system serviced the 120-lot subdivision known as Cool Air. Some of the resort cabins had indoor plumbing, others did not, so a communal bath and shower building was constructed on the southeast corner of what is now Husky and Beresford Way. Sleeper cabins were built with just room for sleeping. There were seven of these in a row above what is now Beresford Court. The total number of cabins, including the sleepers, numbered 23. The road system used to access these cabins is the same one used today. These improvements were done between the years of 1920 to 1934.

By the fall of 1935, the first of the modern lodges with a concrete foundation was finished and in use. This was constructed east of the original Hampton complex where the present day Mineral Lodge sits. The next two lodges were built on this same concrete foundation and porch. Today this porch sags a little in some places, showing its age over the ensuing years. The first Lodge was extremely upscale and modern for its time. It had a beautiful lobby with a massive stone fireplace and a grand staircase going up to the five rooms above, all with private baths. The upstairs also had rooms for employees and a large, two-room apartment for my family—one room for sleeping and another with kitchen, dining, and living space. I remember that when it was first built, my family did not have facilities for bathing and had to walk through a vacant area to take a bath in one of the unused guest rooms. Later this vacant area was finished to add four more rooms, and we even got our own bath tub.

The lobby area was located at the west end of the building. Next to the lobby was the restaurant, referred to as the Coffee Shop. Next in line under the same roof was the grocery store with the Post Office next to it, and at the east end of the building was the bar called the Buffet. All of this was connected with a covered porch. Mounted black-tailed deer heads with large racks of antlers lined the back walls of this porch.

This building burned to the ground September 30, 1939. I was eight years old at the time and playing dress-up with three of my friends when the fire started. We had taken our own clothes

Lobby, c. 1935 (Eastman Studio)

Mineral Lodge, burned 1939 (Eastman Studio)

Remains of the Mineral Lodge after the 1939 fire

off, put on my mother's clothing, and walked across the street in these outfits, even the high-heeled shoes. I can still see the white-strap shoes I had on that day. How I was able to walk any place in them, I can only wonder. It was at this point that the fire started in a chimney flue at the western end of the structure. Once it was discovered, people rushed out to look, leaving the doors opened, so the fire spread rapidly in the wooden structure. Mineral had no fire department at the time. The only assistance was from the National Park Service and Forest Service facilities, but this was a large building, and there was little equipment to fight such a fire. The fire soon spread through the second story; the whole building was consumed in a couple of hours.

Back with my friends in our dress-up clothing and shoes: We had walked across the highway into Cool Air when Kate Phillips saw us and made us come into her house to keep us safe and out of the way. Her husband was the local Highway Patrolman. We had a bird's eye view of the fire, watching the smoke come out from under the eaves and the flames in the windows. I can't quite remember my thoughts during this time, except to recall my friends bemoaning the loss of their clothes, which were upstairs in the burning building and me thinking, "What are they complaining about? I am losing all my clothes and my home." I learned later that my father and others struggled to put out the fire until it became hopeless, then tried to remove what valuable items they could. My father carried out a large cash register that three men could not lift the next day. One man followed my mother upstairs and rescued all the bedding from the three beds plus an armload of clothing. Most of the clothing in this one rescue belonged to me, so I had a few things to wear. But no shoes! I will never forget going to Red Bluff the next day to buy shoes. I had on some old lady's bedroom slippers, the ones with fake wool around the top, ugly and very unsuitable in my eyes. We could not park right in front of the shoe store, so it was a long walk for a vain and embarrassed eight-year old.

Our family moved into the Woodson summer home, originally the Hampton's house and the first hotel in Mineral. This house for

Double hotels, c. 1948 (Eastman Studio)

Double hotel cabin interior, c. 1948 (Eastman Studio)

the time was roomy; it had a large living room, kitchen, bedroom, and bath downstairs, with three small bedrooms, a bath and a large room with an outside entrance upstairs. It was garishly decorated—all of the living room furniture was made of wooden knobs painted black and red. The room upstairs with the outside entrance had every board painted a different color. We called this room the Kitty Parlor for reasons I can't recall. As my mother was the postmaster, we had the Post Office in the corner of our living room with an outside window for customers. The Mineral Lodge was under contract to feed the extra state highway employees who were needed in times of stormy weather, so my mother now had to feed them when it was necessary. When I think about it, this must had been quite a burden on her, but I don't remember her ever complaining. Her German work ethic came shining through. My mother had purchased her first wringer-washing machine on credit from good old Montgomery Wards before the fire. The machine burned up, and she had to replace it—and now pay for two.

It was a very low time for our family. We had lost the business that supported us and did not have sufficient funds to rebuild. Certain images remain in my mind from this period. I can see my mother trying to be comfortable on a five-foot wooden couch that was only 18 inches wide with 12 inches of thin padding and a straight wooden back. Things improved little by little as people gave us replacements for what we had lost, and we soldiered on.

Motel with covered parking built in 1940 (Eastman Studio)

Irreplaceable items such as pictures of my brother and me were lost forever. When I was about twelve, a relative sent copies of some of my baby pictures. I was so thrilled with these pictures that I went around showing them to everyone until one woman said "My, what an ugly child." I was very careful to whom I showed the pictures after that.

In order to rebuild the Lodge, my father decided to sell the timber on the land surrounding the building. This was virgin timber that had never been logged before and would provide the necessary funds. As there was no lumber mill in Mineral, he persuaded Sam Crowley, who operated a mill in Quincy, to move his mill to Mineral. From then on, the Mineral Mill and logging became a good part of our life.

The next Lodge building was rebuilt in the spring of 1940 using the same foundation as the previous Lodge, but it was not as luxurious due to the shortage of funds. There were no rooms for overnight guests in this Lodge. It had the same covered porch with the mounted deer heads like the previous building. The restaurant was located at the western end where the former lobby had been, next

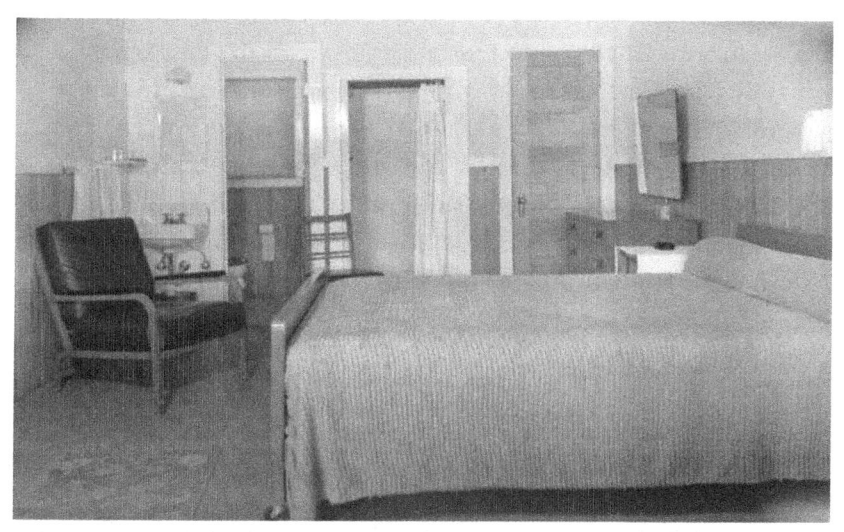

Motel interior built in 1940 (Eastman Studio)

Mineral Lodge room

came the Buffet or bar. Behind the bar was a room connected to the restaurant kitchen where private groups could be served. Next in line was a large unfurnished room used for meetings and dances for guests and the community. This also served as recreation room with a portable Ping-Pong table. Restrooms were located at the back of this room with a hall connected to an office and the Post Office. The only telephone service in Mineral at that time was adjacent to the Post Office window that occupied a corner of the grocery store, which was last in line at the east end of the building. This Lodge was certainly practical, but not sumptuous. A full-sized, fire hydrant with regulation fire hose was installed behind this building as defense against any future fires. At this time, five of the small cabins behind the Lodge were remodeled and upgraded to what we called motel cabins, replacing the hotel rooms that had burned.

In 1940, ten more motel rooms were built west of the Lodge. These were typical of that era with covered parking between each two units. They had one unique feature which was my father's design: The shower and wash basin were at the back of the room with a

New housekeeping cabins, c. 1948 (Eastman Studio)

New housekeeping cabin interior, c. 1949 (Eastman Studio)

separate room for the toilet. People often complained about having to step out into the room from the shower with no clothes on. This concept had not entered my father's mind since he had no modesty.

Mineral Lodge, which burned 1949 (Eastman Studio)

He thought nothing of walking around the whole house naked as he was dressing. One time when he was fishing on Mill Creek with my husband George, Husky slipped and yelled to let George know he was falling. Consequently he lost his teeth and his glasses. Fred's wife, Sue, told me she was going to see how my father was, as she was very fond of him. I said, "Be careful he may not have any clothes on." She returned from the visit a little shocked and said, "You were right."

Following the end of World War II, six additional cabins were built in a row behind the first row of cabins. These we called new housekeeping cabins as they were larger than the original cabins built by Hampton, but still tiny compared to anything today. They had two bedrooms with a bath in between and a nice porch along the front. At the same time, the small, sleeper cabins were taken down as they had no further use. The larger, newer cabins were very popular with our customers for several years.

The second Lodge served the public and our family well until it was also destroyed by a fire on January 10, 1949. It was a bitter cold

SnoGo rotary snow plow (Eastman Studio)

night with the temperature at 0 to -5 degrees below zero and wind gusts of 50 miles an hour. Mineral was used to weather like this but not prepared for a fire in the largest structure in town. At 1:30 a.m. Erma Fields, who lived across the street from the Lodge in Cool Air, saw fire at the east end of the building. Her husband, Hugh, ran across the field to warn the two couples who were staying in the motel cabins west of the Lodge while Edna called Paul Becker, my father, and others who had telephones. Paul Becker was able to get the fire hose on the motel cabins that were already smoking and save them from burning. The fire spread so rapidly and burned with such intensity that the corrugated iron on the roof turned blue and glowed with a flame six inches high. The cold was so intense that, at one time, the water in the fire hose froze under full pressure. There was a small kink in the line that had to be uncoupled to free the line. Firefighting equipment from the National Park Service and the U. S. Forest Service assisted in saving the motel and some nearby cabins, but the main lodge building could not be saved. The whole community turned out to fight the fire and do what they could to help. Women from the community served coffee to everyone during the night.

As people began to relax, another fire was discovered in a garage of the Crowley home in Cool Air. By this time, the water supply had been exhausted and the water lines frozen. The National Park Service used their SnoGo to save the Crowley home by throwing snow on the building and the burning garage. With two fires in one night, the community became alarmed that there might be an arsonist in town until they realized that telephones were involved. The fire in the Lodge had started in the area where the telephone was located, and the Crowley Garage, used as an office, also had a telephone. Everyone who had a telephone went home and cut their lines. This was indeed the problem, or part of the problem. A tree, less than a mile west of the Lodge, had fallen on a PG&E 11,000-volt line that in turn fell across the Citizens Utility's telephone line which shorted-out the switchboard at the Lodge. The snow on the ground was so frozen that it supported the weight of the tree and did not shut off the current. A truck had come up the highway before the Crowley fire and tangled the low-hanging lines, thus causing the second fire.

The *Red Bluff Daily News* article of January 10, 1949, describing the Lodge fire had this to say:

> *If everyone who felt sorry about the Mineral fire started up the mountain to extend a hand of sympathy to Katie and Husky Beresford, there'd be a solid line of traffic from here to there, from now to then . . . . So the Red Bluff Daily News is taking upon itself the task of telling the Beresfords how sorry all of Tehama is. It is a tough break. We're all sorry. We hope that the Beresfords have the courage to rebuild. We're sure they will. They're that kind of people. And Mineral Lodge has always been one of the things we're proudest of down here in the valley. It couldn't have happened to two sweller people.*

This was a great tribute to my parents and their years of service to the public.

By the middle of July 1950, the Mineral Lodge reopened as it stands today. It is three buildings constructed of cinder block. My parents were not about to put all their eggs in one basket again; the cinder block was double insurance. The first building was used as an office and lobby. The second building housed the bar and restaurant, and the third the grocery store. A small building between the restaurant and grocery store was the Post Office and office. While the second fire was certainly not good, it was not the great disaster like the first fire because we had better fire insurance. One insurance policy paid all the employees' salaries while the business was not operating. This made it possible for the business to be down for the six months it took to rebuild and reopen again with the same key employees. With ample funds for rebuilding, we opened with the latest and best equipment for the day. The restaurant kitchen was designed and furnished by Nathan Dorman, a prestigious restaurant supplier from San Francisco. The bar was designed by Don Carver who had designed the Palomino Room in Red Bluff. Due to this special design, it was called The Rafter Room. It has been a challenge ever since for men to try to swing from one side of the room to the other on the rafters after a few drinks. My brother, Fred, was one of the few who could accomplish this feat, which was not easy because the rafters are 4 x 4s with sharp edges. The lobby was furnished with nice easy chairs and an impressive, large flagstone fireplace with the addition of a gift shop in the front half of the building. That first year, my father purchased the gift shop inventory, but after that, it became my responsibility. For 30 years I had great fun attending the Gift Show in either San Francisco or Los Angeles, purchasing many different items and jewelry. I am not sure the Gift Shop made much money, but it was a big attraction for all the guests. The grocery store was also well equipped with the latest in refrigeration and shelving.

The aftermath of the second Lodge fire was that, on November 6, 1951, my parents brought suit against PG&E and the Citizens Utility Company to recover the $100,000 loss of the lodge building. A jury trial in Tehama County lasted over six weeks with 22 court days. It was the longest civil case to be tried in that court up to that time. The jury awarded my parents $102,947 on December 13, 1951. Nine jurors voted for the award and three did not. Civil cases do not have to have a unanimous decision. The judge had excused the Citizens Utility Company early in the trial.

This decision was considered a landmark case for many years because it involved expert testimony against a large corporation. The expert witnesses were electrical engineers from the University of California at Berkeley, and the case was won when the engineers were able to ignite a fire on a piece of wood in the court room using the voltage of the PG&E line. The verdict was appealed through the upper courts for the next four years. Each time the original verdict was upheld. Finally PG&E paid the award plus interest, and my parents had money in the bank for the first time.

During my senior year at college, I was introduced to a law student, who said, "Beresford—are you related to the people who sued PG&E?" I said, "Yes," and we had a long conversation concerning the case. ⁕

Present Mineral Lodge (Eastman Studio)

CHAPTER 7

THE STORE

Mineral Lodge expanded and contracted over the 120 years of its operation with various businesses. The most important part of the resort, in my opinion, was the grocery store, which we called the Store. The Store sold everything from plumbing supplies to T-bone steaks. There was nothing put on the shelves that did not sell at some time or another. Mineral Lodge had many employees over the years; some worked only a few days or weeks, but many of them worked for years. Two of the most important employees were the Woodwards, Merrill and his wife, Floy. Merrill managed the Store, and Floy did the laundry for the motel units and cabins. Merrill started working in Mineral sometime around 1920 when my father picked him up as a hitchhiker and subsequently offered him a job. He worked until 1964 when he and Floy retired to their new home in Red Bluff. In the years between, they gave their hearts and souls, along with a spectacular work ethic, to Mineral Lodge.

Both Merrill and Floy came from early pioneer families in Tehama County. Merrill's grandfather, Abner Nanny, settled in Paynes Creek. The family was musical and played for neighborhood dances. One of Abner's daughters, Ida, married Richard Lincoln Woodward of Lanes Valley where they raised 12 children; Merrill being next to the oldest. Floy's family, the Wrights, settled in Manton with eight children; Floy was the oldest. With the many children in their respective families and the distance to Red Bluff, neither Floy nor Merrill finished high school. Both of them wanted more for their two children, Marilyn and Dick. Dick graduated from the University of California at Berkeley and went on to teach high school in Fremont. Marilyn attended business school and always commanded good jobs wherever she lived. They both appreciated what their parents gave them.

In the early years of Mineral Lodge, when it was called Mineral Camp Site, everyone did everything; Merrill was the lead man. He worked in the Store, broke horses, chopped wood, milked cows, cut meat, and did a sundry of other things. One of my earliest memories of Merrill is when he was at the top of a pine tree over 100 feet tall and having trouble getting to the ground. It was the practice to cut the top off of these tall pines in the hope that this would keep them from blowing over in high winds. Merrill had successfully topped the tree, and everyone was concerned as to how to get him down. How he did, I do not remember, but imagine climbing up that high and sawing off the top five or six feet of a tree by yourself. As I remember, this was the last of some six or seven trees he had successfully topped. Wood was the main source of heat in the early years, and Merrill did most of the collecting work—from felling the trees to stacking the wood. I remember an area of stacked wood the size of a football field available every fall.

The Store was typical of an old-time, country store. The counter and cash register were at the back of room. All the liquor was behind the counter for safekeeping. There was a walk-in refrigerator where all meat, milk, ice, and related cool products were stored. The cool products had to be loaded in deli-like cases as needed. Ice was delivered in large 300 pound blocks that were scored in sections that weighed 25 pounds each. To sell a block of ice, one used an ice pick to get a smaller piece off the main block, lift the small piece by tongs, put it in a cardboard container, and carry it to the counter—not an easy or time efficient job.

Hampton's Mineral Store (courtesy Dan Foster)

Meat was purchased by half a cow, referred to as a side-of-beef. Merrill was the butcher. The Store was noted for its excellent steaks and other cuts of meat. Merrill would also cut special orders for people.

The Store was well stocked with groceries of every variety. If you wanted a can of pineapple, you had your choice of crushed or sliced, large or small. All varieties of beer, soft drinks, potato chips, bread, pastries, and dairy products were available for purchase. The Store carried plumbing, hardware, and fishing equipment—from live worms to fishing poles. You name it, the Store usually had it available. It was really a 7–11 ahead of its time. Merrill took care of all of this with extra help in the summer months.

Against one wall was a small area of magazines for sale. The lower portion was devoted to what we called funny books, referred to today as comics. I spent many hours sitting here reading the funny books. I remember the first Wonder Woman comic, which I thought was needed for girls to read.

Interior of the store, c. 1949 (Eastman Studio)

In the winter, the Store rented skis. There were over 60 pair with boots and poles to match. The skis were painted bright red with large, black numbers on the tips to discourage theft. Merrill rented all of these by himself on busy weekends.

One unique feature of the Store concerned credit: Members of the community could charge their purchases. The charges were written by hand with one copy for the purchaser and one for the business. The total was billed at the end of the month and paid any time after that. I am sure this was standard practice with some businesses when credit cards did not yet exist. But, at the Store, there was a second type of credit extended to anybody at any time. There were no set rules, except that it probably did not apply to the regular charge customers. If a customer did not have the cash at the time of purchase, he signed the small sales tag, and it was Scotch–taped vertically to one side of the shelf that held the liquor. These small 2 x 2 inch slips stayed there until the purchaser returned and paid the amount. The whole system was based on trust and promise, and it

Interior of the store, c. 1965 (Eastman Studio)

worked amazingly well. Most people paid in a relatively short time, and some people came back two years later to pay their slip—very few never paid. I remember these small slips of paper always being there. Merrill's son, Dick, told me that there were usually more than 100 of them. Early day credit cards.

My brother, Fred, went to work in the Store when he was 11; Dick started working that same year when he was nine. Both of them continued working there weekends and vacations until they graduated from the university. Both were excellent employees because Merrill was a strict and benevolent teacher, and they were eager to learn.

One good story concerns both boys: While in their teens, they and their friends had some rip-roaring camp outs in the summer months. Fred and Dick supplied the liquor and cigarettes for these affairs, which usually occurred three or four times a summer. Merrill opened the Store at 7:00 a.m. and closed at 10:00 p.m. He did not take a lunch hour, but went home to dinner at 5:30 for half an hour. This was the time for the boys' friends to come load up the goods for the evening's fun.

The boys themselves never paid for the booze, yet the Store got its money. You might wonder how this was accomplished. It was an elaborate system that the boys learned from Merrill himself. During World War II, businesses were not allowed to raise their prices. This put the Store in somewhat of a pickle because some of the goods had to be freighted in on the stage that operated between Red Bluff and Susanville. The ration board did not allow the price of the freight to be added to the selling price. This meant lost money on those items. To make up the lost funds, Merrill taught the boys to take the bottom reading on the scale of anything they weighed—the reading that first registered when the weight of an item caused the scale to drop before it rose to the actual reading—and keep track of this amount until they made up the difference he asked them to. However, at the time of these camp outs, the war was over and price controls were long gone, so that maneuver was no longer necessary—but the boys used it to pay for their fun. They kept strict records in a small notebook hidden from Merrill in which every penny was accounted for.

There is an interesting story concerning Dick and my good friend Rosemary's mother, Nell. Nell was very frugal, watching every penny she spent. I remember her sitting on the front porch of the Lodge adding up in her head the adding machine tape that had been included in her monthly bill from the Store. I do not remember that she ever challenged the bill. One time when Rosemary was in college and Dick was in high school, Nell came into the Store to purchase some lettuce. She and Rosemary had been staying in a cabin for spring vacation and were ready to go home in two days. She asked Dick for a small head of lettuce. At that time, all the lettuce was kept in the walk-in refrigerator. Dick had to bring it out to her so she could pass judgment for proper size. After she had refused five or six heads of lettuce as being too large, Dick, who was well-steeped in pleasing the customer, took off two or three of the outside leafs of a head of lettuce and presented it to her. She was very pleased, saying that was just what she wanted, how much was the price? Dick's business-like reply was, "21 cents. All of our heads of lettuce are 21 cents." She paid the price and told the story herself.

To earn extra money, Merrill contracted to cut Christmas trees to sell in bulk to wholesalers. He would buy them from a local landowner, cut and stack them, then sell them to the best buyer he could find. The first year of his tree operation, he hired his daughter, Marilyn, and me to cut trees for 10 cents each. It was such hard work, I only did it once. I was maybe 10 or 11 and weighed less than 70 pounds—lugging a five-foot fir tree anyplace was no fun. That was the end of my Christmas tree career, but it inspired my brother, Fred. He spent most of his life growing and selling Christmas trees and loved every minute of it. Merrill was Fred's role model. Fred told me that if he ever thought of not getting up on a snowy day, he would think, "What would Merrill do?" The answer was: Merrill would get up and attack the day. Fred acted accordingly.

In addition to their work in the Store, Merrill and Floy farmed on the side. They kept eight to ten milk cows in the summer, supplying milk and cream for sale in the Store. This meant milking the cows

Joan Beresford, Carol Jean Ellis, and Merrill Woodward on a trip to Turner Mountain

twice a day, separating the cream, and bottling the milk. Raw milk was declared unsafe in the middle of World War II, but the Store kept selling it because we had the problem of the extra expense of freight from Red Bluff. One day, officials discovered we were still selling raw milk and colored all the milk blue so it could not be sold. After this episode we were able to raise the price of milk that was shipped in. I remember being so embarrassed by this episode; now I know it was the only way to solve the price freeze and shipping problem. Merrill also raised pigs, feeding them the slop from the Coffee Shop until that became illegal. Pigs could only eat cooked food. I feel like I grew up on a farm because of Merrill as he raised sheep, too. I even was able to watch him butcher these animals.

Floy's contributions were equally as valuable. When raw milk was banned and she no longer had the cows to milk, Floy took on the laundry of the Lodge's motel units and cabins. She did this in her own home, starting with wringer washers to wash and clotheslines to dry. In later years, better equipment made her job easier, but imagine all the sheets and towels for 20 motel units and 14 cabins in the busy summer months. She worked hard at this for 15 years. It was no wonder that her heart gave out fairly early in her life.

In addition to being exceptionally hard workers, Merrill and Floy were lovely people. They never had a bad word to say about anybody. If one of their many sisters, brothers, or neighbors needed help, Merrill and Floy were there. Floy took care of an elderly pioneer couple by the name of Moon until they died. The Moons had a cabin in Mineral with no children to help them. They left Floy some money because they could, but she would have cared for them regardless of their financial status. Merrill was always upbeat. He never complained and always looked on the bright side of life. He did have one quirk: He always told the customers the weather report they wanted to hear, regardless of what it truly was. I believe he developed this over the years of dealing with the public because he did not want to hear customers complain if the weather did not suit their plans.

At retirement in 1964, Merrill and Floy moved to Red Bluff. They purchased 20 acres on Live Oak Road where they built a lovely home. Merrill raised a few cattle and butchered meat for his many friends and clients. Floy died before Merrill from her bad heart. Marilyn, their daughter, told me that she was so grateful for the TV soap "As the World Turns" because her father sat down every afternoon with a beer to watch the program. He never sat down in the middle of a day for anything else in his life. Another good story involved Merrill's and Floy's 50th wedding anniversary in Reno with the whole family. After a fancy dinner and late-night activities, Merrill said he would meet the rest of the family for breakfast. They were surprised when he called at 6:00 a.m. His explanation was that 6:00 a.m. was when he always ate breakfast. Merrill died at age 86. He had delivered a calf two days before his death—working to the end and happy for it.

After Merrill retired, Dick managed the Store the summer of 1964, then my brother, Fred, took over. Fred did an excellent job, but his heart was not in it. He was not a people-person, and the constant pressure of the public did not suit him. He had become interested in growing Christmas trees and wanted to spend his time outdoors, planting and growing trees.

In 1968, to accommodate Fred and to accumulate what we hoped would be a good retirement income, my husband, George, and I, along with Fred and his wife, Sue, purchased 160 acres near Paynes Creek for a tree farm. The elevation was 3,000 feet, and a good portion of the land had been leveled for use as a landing field—good for the planting of Christmas trees. The property also had a small house, a water system, and a couple who had been caretakers for a several years.

Our plan was to have Fred continue in the Store during the summer months, and the other three of us would fill in most of the time during the spring, fall, and winter. This worked quite well. I took over the weekly ordering of supplies for the Store except for the liquor, which George did in connection with the bar. Sue and I took turns working in the Store during the week; Fred still worked busy weekends. The checkout stand and cash register had been moved to the front of the Store for a more modern approach. We still operated the Store as Merrill had, stocking a good supply of hardware, fishing supplies, and all items found in most grocery stores from milk to potato chips.

Sue and I had a few scary times, especially in the winter. We stayed open until 6:00 p.m. to accommodate local employees and travelers, which meant it was pretty dark when we closed up. Putting the money in the floor safe after we locked the door was always a trauma if we had a customer that late, as we often did. Steve Jones owned and operated Mt. Lassen Motor Transit. He delivered papers to us in the morning and returned late in the afternoon, often with two or more released felons from the Susanville State Prison. Steve always put us on the alert. The felons were never any trouble, probably because Mineral was no place they wanted to be, and there were usually other customers around. I always tried to do some bookwork when I was in the Store, but this was nearly impossible because someone was always coming in the front door. The parking lot very seldom had only our vehicle parked there.

This system of shared workload worked pretty well for a few years until George took over a ski rental business in South Lake Tahoe and was not around to help us. So in 1970 we leased the Store to John Dennis. John had worked most of his life for large chain grocery stores; their management style really did not fit into how we had operated the Store over the years. Their emphasis was based on how fast or slow items were sold. John operated the Store accordingly. His stock was mostly sodas, beer, potato chips, and candy. He was his own delivery man, driving to Red Bluff or Redding to pick up his merchandise. Naturally, the sales volume went down. I just can't remember whether it was profitable for us as landlords or how successful John was. John became bored with Mineral and the Store and asked to be let out of his lease in 1977. By this time I was the only family member interested in the Mineral Lodge, and I was happy to release him.

I took over running the Store that spring and stocked it according to how Merrill had operated all those many years before. I had the shelves loaded to the gills, and people were lined up 10 and 12 deep several times a day purchasing what they needed. Everyone who had not been around for a few years thought I was a genius, but the credit really went to Merrill. I was just a copycat.

Coffee Shop with Jo Ann Perkins and waitresses (Eastman Studio)

CHAPTER 8

THE COFFEE SHOP

I was thrilled to go to work in the Coffee Shop at age 13. The year was 1944 with World War II raging and all available men and women were employed in the war effort. I believe that was the reason I was employable at that early age. I washed dishes one week and waited on tables the next week. I shared this responsibility with my friend, Carol Jean Ellis, who was also 13. We were required to wear a white uniform and apron. I was usually pretty messy looking at the end of a shift, and to this day I never wear white clothing. As I remember, we only worked the breakfast shift which meant getting up when it was dark in order to arrive at 5:30 a.m. I have never liked getting out of bed when it is dark since. The Mineral Mill was in full operation providing lumber for bomb racks with the majority of the employees single men living in the Mineral Lodge's various cabins and eating their meals in the restaurant. We served between 20 and 25 men at breakfast and also packed lunches for them. This was a hardworking, rough group of men, but I do not remember receiving anything but respect from them. I very definitely learned how to be a waitress and what hard work was all about.

Mineral Lodge always had a full-service restaurant, serving breakfast, lunch, and dinner but it was always referred to as the

Coffee Shop. All of Mineral Lodge was open seven days a week, all year long. For as long as I can remember, the kitchen help was Chinese and remained so until sometime in the 1960s. The Chinese were hired through employment agencies in San Francisco. They liked working in Mineral because they could save money since their salary included room and board. My father hired them because, if they quit, they would not leave the job until a replacement arrived. Depending on the season, we usually had between two and four Chinese in the kitchen. They never took a day off and were wonderful employees, hardworking and good natured unless they were under pressure with a lot of customers. They were wonderful cooks—made all of their own everything including soups, sauces, pies, cakes, and dinner rolls. During those years, Mineral Lodge had a reputation for excellent food. Sunday dinners were usually crowded with people from the valley. The Chinese food they made for themselves was very good, and I loved eating with them except when they served pig's head or thousand-year-old eggs, which were their favorites.

The Chinese were the absolute bosses of the kitchen, starting with the chief cook to the dishwasher. You did what they told you to do, and there was no back talk. They were seldom wrong, but even if they were, you did not dispute their orders. When they said, "chop-chop," you "chopped-chopped" as quickly as you could. My friend, Marilyn Woodward, had an experience she will never forget. She was waiting table during a very busy dinner hour. The veal cutlet slid off the plate as she removed it from the order counter. The dishwasher hurriedly picked it up off the floor, put it back on the plate, and told her to serve it. She did with great reluctance because she knew she could not say no, even to the dishwasher. This was a rare occurrence in the kitchen.

Charley Yee was the chief cook when I started my career as a waitress. He had been with us several years and planned to retire and return home to China as a rich man with the money he had saved over the years. At that time, this was the goal for most Chinese working in America. World War II had delayed his plans, so he was not able to leave for home until early 1946. My father was driving him to Red Bluff to catch a bus to San Francisco for the plane trip back to China when he asked, "Charley, I bet you have 90 cents for every dollar I have paid you over the years." The reply was "No, no, Mr. Blesford, I have 99 cents." Unfortunately for Charley, life did not work out as he had planned. The Chinese Communists took his money, and he had to return to the United States a poor man. We gave him a job as a dishwasher. He was 85 at the time and too old to be the chief cook. He could not keep his mouth shut and kept trying to tell the current chef how to do it his way or something like that. Finally, the current chef said he was leaving unless we fired Charley. By this time I was mainly in charge of the restaurant, and I had to tell Charley it was not working out. I can still see the sad face of the man who had given us so much service. He did have a son in Stockton, so he was not homeless. But it was a sad experience for us all.

One other chief cook—we did not refer to them as chefs—I distinctly remember was Frank Toy who was a large man with a pocked face. He would not allow me to come into the kitchen with shorts on; women were to wear dresses in his book. He would put his hand in his pocket and hand me a $10 bill saying "Go buy good clothes." Like most Chinese he loved to gamble and would take the stage to Susanville and on to Reno for a few days. I do not remember if he ever came home with a lot of money.

Albert Chan was our all-time favorite chief cook who probably stayed the longest. He was only 28 when he came to work for us, but looked like a teenager. After he had been there for a few years, he went to China and returned to Mineral with a wife. This was a new experience for all of us. Florence was very quiet but all smiles. She had four little girls in the next six years. Albert and Florence left Mineral in 1955; he had relatives in San Francisco who wanted him to take over their restaurant. Florence wrote to us two or three years later saying that Albert had died. We were all saddened by this news. But that is not the end of the story of the Chans.

Albert and Florence Chan, Wong, and three Chan children

I had moved back to Mineral in 1989 after working in Sacramento for five years, when I got a telephone call from Judy Chan who was staying at Mineral Lodge for the weekend. She was the eldest of Albert's children and remembered living in Mineral and wanted to talk to me about her father. She was only eight or nine when he died, and her mother never talked about her father. She wanted to know more about him and hoped I could help her out. Since that time, the Chans have been to Mineral several times—mother Florence, daughter's Judy, Janet, and Janice along with their husbands. The third daughter died when she was 15. She never looked as healthy as the others because she carried the gene of sickle cell anemia. Apparently there is a strain of this disease in China as in Africa. All three remaining daughters have the same personality as their father, very gregarious, happy, and lots of fun. It has been a very rewarding experience to know them.

The only Chinese words I ever learned were "Chop! Chop!" (Hurry up) and "Jun ne-ga how nau" (I'll chop your head off). On one of the Chan's visits to Mineral, Florence read an early draft of this book and set me straight how to spell and pronounce "I'll chop your head off."

"All young Chinese man wants to work in Post Office," said one old Chinese cook, and he was certainly correct. Later we could not find any Chinese willing to come to an out-of-the-way place like Mineral. But here came the Filipinos. They were also excellent cooks as most of them had worked for the U.S. Navy in food service. They were quite willing to come to Mineral. Angelo was my first Filipino chef. By this time, I had more or less taken charge of the Coffee Shop. This meant designing the menu, ordering the food, hiring all of the help, and waiting on tables when necessary. I was able to do that fairly easily because I had always been there and had grown up with the place. But I did not know how to cook! I did not even know how to cook when I got married at age 24 because my family had always eaten in the restaurant. I had learned, sort of, to cook for my husband, but restaurant cooking was a whole different ball game. In the back of my mind, I knew that sooner or later someone in the family would have to learn more about that part of the business. I also knew that I was that someone.

My first attempt in the Mineral Lodge kitchen was rather a disaster. It was late in the fall, and the Restaurant was closed for the month of November and most of December until Christmas time and the skiing began. We had rented some motel cabins to a church group of 30 people for a weekend retreat, and they needed to eat. I quoted them a price for lodging and three meals, dinner, breakfast, and lunch. I had myself and my sister-in-law, Sue, to handle the situation. How we handled the dinner I do not remember, but I will never forget the breakfast. We were serving bacon and scrambled eggs. The kitchen had a gas grill about 48 x 36 inches with a gutter in front to take away any excess grease. The excess grease flowed into a vertical container at the end of the grill. We started cooking the bacon on this grill, 90 pieces of bacon. All was going great until the container for the excess grease began to overflow all over the kitchen floor. Usually the container was easy to remove and empty but not when it was filled with hot bacon grease. I do not think I even knew about the excess grease container, let alone think to empty it first. How we solved the situation, I am not sure, but we did get the breakfast served on time and did not burn the eggs or the bacon.

Now back to Angelo, my first Filipino chef. He worked in Mineral for five or six years, and he really taught me how to cook. Under his leadership, we established a buffet dinner on Saturday nights during the months of June, July, and August. This buffet was quite spectacular; we served prime rib, fried chicken, large marinated shrimp, deep-fried chicken livers wrapped in bacon, melon balls served in a carved watermelon basket, and several ring-molded salads. The desserts were also wonderful—cheesecake, black bottom pie, meringue sundae, and a good selection of pies. Some of my

Angelo

The buffet

family contributed their part. George donned a chef's uniform and carved the prime rib, which we served last after everyone's plate was full of other food. Angelo taught us to cook fried chicken that melted in your mouth. Sue and I did the chicken, four large trays each week. We also did the melon balls. My mother made the molded salads, and I made the cheesecakes. To this day, family holidays only have this cheesecake for dessert—we would not consider anything else. I believe we charged $3.50 for this repast, but remember, this was 1968. Still it was a real bargain. Angelo was boss in the kitchen, and we were good friends. I certainly learned a lot from him.

The Chinese were big gamblers, and some of the Filipinos were drinkers. Angelo liked his liquor, and, though he was not drunk all the time, he had his moments. When he would bow to me and call me "Madame So Lay," I knew we were in for trouble. I would have to cook for a day or so until he sobered up. Finally, after six years of this, and I knew how to cook well enough by then, I fired him! He knew he had pushed the button too far. But it was a sad day for us both.

Bernie was another of my great Filipino cooks. He lived in South San Francisco with a family of four boys. For a good five years he worked every summer, continuing on with the buffet, but his best dish was pot roast with potato pancakes. The pancakes melted in your mouth; I can still taste them. Bernie had the best temperament of any cook I ever hired. He never got excited, he did not drink or gamble, and he was a perfect gentlemen. I missed his kind soul when he could not come back one summer because of his age.

Pete was a young Filipino who worked for a couple of summers. He was a good cook, and he loved to decorate the plates. He carved potatoes that looked like roses and many other flowers out of carrots and other vegetables. The appetizing appearance of the summer buffet was a sight to behold when he was working. He had a wife and two or three children, so I housed them in the old Hampton hotel one summer. This was two stories with a large living room on the first floor. Pete and his family were not comfortable because there was too much space. They had never lived in anything that large before, so they all lived in one room and felt safe that way. I missed having Pete and his family as I never heard from them after that summer. The big house scared them away I guess.

Interesting things always happen when you deal with the public. One occasion I remember very vividly is the man who exited the restroom, through the kitchen, with a long trail of toilet paper streaming behind him. As he exited the front door, it cut off the toilet paper, and he left never knowing he had caused a great sensation and peals of laughter.

The last ten years of operating the Coffee Shop were the hardest. I could no longer hire the Filipinos or the Chinese. Fortunately, there were some local women who were excellent cooks. Marge Rudolph was a gem. She waited tables and filled in as cook whenever necessary, until she became the full-time cook. Her chili beans and soup were wonderful. Between the two of us we managed the buffet using all the knowledge we had gained from all the chefs. One of the biggest obstacles was the size of the kitchen. It had been designed by the San Francisco Nathan Dorman Company in 1949 for a different era. It measured 20 x 30 feet and was not designed well, as it was far too large and required more employees than we could afford. I remodeled it for a more efficient operation.

One funny story concerning this remodel project involved an exhaust fan above the existing grill. I was moving the grill and all its equipment up to the front of the kitchen and moving the fan back against another wall. The health inspector said I could not use the old fan; too old and inefficient he said. The contractor, John Lewis, a good friend, took the fan and had it repainted a different color. The inspector approved the new fan. That fan is still working as far as I know. I still smile when I think of that coup.

We ultimately sold the Coffee Shop and Bar business with the buildings to Irene and Chuck Kindig. Chuck was a good cook, and Irene was a super promoter. They were very successful, and both families worked well together until we put all the businesses back together in 1980. It was a good real estate market and a good time to sell. The resort business, especially a restaurant, are time consuming and a lot of hard work with no guarantees of financial success. Life with the Mineral Lodge had been fun and very educational, but it was time to move on and enjoy the flowers.

We did sell the resort to the George McKeenan family in 1980, who then sold it to Larry and Julien Eklington in 1988, who later sold to Beth and Jim Glenn in 1996. The Glenns still own and operate it with their family. I have been free as a bird with lots of great memories ever since. ℰ𝒪

Mineral Lodge Coffee Shop, c. 1949 (Eastman Studio)

Mineral Lodge Coffee Shop, c. 1937 (Eastman Studio)

HOLIDAYS

Thanksgiving in my Family

Until I was 27, I only remember one Thanksgiving dinner with a large family present. I grew up eating most, if not all, my meals in the Mineral Lodge Coffee Shop, and Thanksgiving was no exception. My father usually ate his evening meal at 5:00 p.m., and he did not vary this routine for any holiday. The lodge restaurant served excellent food, and it should have as there were always four Chinese working in the kitchen—a chef, his assistant, sous chef, and a dishwasher. The traditional Thanksgiving meal was served with all the trimmings—turkey, mashed potatoes, gravy, homemade dressing, shrimp cocktail, homemade rolls, pumpkin or mincemeat pie, and plum pudding with hard sauce. Our small family—my mother, father, and brother, Fred—sat together for this holiday fare until I went to work in the restaurant at age 13 and my brother in the grocery store when he was 11. After that, we ate together when we could, but if either Fred or I were working when our parents had their five o'clock dinner, we did not join them. We had our dinner when we were through with our jobs and usually ate with the employees we worked with. The large family dinner I remember was in Corning when I was around seven or eight. I was visiting my Grandmother Nellie Victoria, my father's mother. The dinner was with her relatives, the Baldersons and Rochfords. Neither of my parents were present as they were busy in Mineral.

This Thanksgiving routine went on until Fred married Sue and they moved to Mineral. Her mother served the traditional Thanksgiving dinner in Colusa with cut flowers, Lenox china, sterling silver, and everyone dressed to the nines. By this time, Fred was into the Christmas tree business, and this was his busy time. He had a hard time showing up in Colusa because his trees were in Mineral. It only took a few years for Sue's mother, Elizabeth, to figure out that if she wanted a family Thanksgiving dinner, it had to be in Mineral. I believe Fred did not show up in Colusa on time, or did not show up at all after the first or second year. Elizabeth was a trooper. She brought the whole trappings and trimmings to Fred's and Sue's house in Mineral. My family, including my mother, was included as we were family. My father had passed away, and the Mineral Lodge was no longer open at this time of year.

This first dinner was wonderful—the food superb, turkey cooked to perfection, and a congenial group. This was the first time I had ever heard of having the turkey cooked so it was not too dry. I just thought you just cooked it. Since Elizabeth and Hap, her husband, had cooked the dinner, it was my job to clean up. What a nightmare! The kitchen was small with no dishwasher, they had not cleaned up as they went along, every dish was used, and on and on. It took my mother and me over two hours to successfully finish the job. It did not take me long to decide that they could cook the turkey however they wanted, but we were eating it at my house; I had a bigger kitchen with a dishwasher, and I cleaned up as I cooked—I had watched those Chinese for years.

So for the next several years, we had great Thanksgivings—they cooked the turkey, and we ate at my house. Then, sadly, Elizabeth died, and there we were with no one to cook the turkey. Neither my mother nor Sue nor I knew how to cook a turkey let alone know if it was too dry or whatever. The first year we left the giblets inside the turkey in the plastic bag and did not discover our error until we carved the bird. We did not do that the second year, but we had a hard time knowing when the turkey was done. The third year, we drank too much waiting for the turkey to finish cooking. After that, we shaped up and things went along smoothly for our Thanksgivings.

Please note that I cooked Thanksgiving dinner for over 100 people when I had my Red Bluff restaurant, "The Victorian," in 1983.

Christmas

I described Thanksgivings for the Beresford family as they became more traditional, but Christmases were another matter. I have pleasant memories of Christmas in my childhood, but I doubt if they would be considered traditional. I guess the best part of our holidays is that I am not left with any hang-ups concerning Christmas. I do not feel any stress at that period of the year, mainly because I am not pressured to have this done or that done. People ask me if I am ready for Christmas, I always

Beresford family Christmas, c. 1950

say, "Of course I am." I do not bother to tell them I don't care if I am ready or not and that it makes no difference to me one way or the other. I also have no great expectations concerning Christmas, so I don't feel let down when the holidays are over.

You might be left with the impression that my family did not have Christmas. We did, but it was very low-key. My mother did not like to decorate the tree, but she made sure there were plenty of ornaments, lights, and tinsel. My father always made sure there was a tree. It was always a silvertip. The red fir or silvertip trees have large spaces between the limbs, usually 8 to 10 inches. This species of fir is still considered premium and demands the highest price in Christmas tree lots today. My father would bring the tree in the house three or four days before Christmas. Fred and I and my father would then decorate it. That was it for Christmas decorations. Who needed more? Both parents made sure there were presents under the tree for my brother and me, not a lot, but enough. Sometime there was clothing for winter use and usually a new pair of skies if we needed them that year.

My mother always made divinity candy, which was her specialty. This homemade candy is difficult as it can go to sugar easily if not prepared exactly right. She also made Christmas cookies in two or three varieties. Sometimes she was too busy to have all this ready for Christmas and if she didn't, she did it later, or not at all. Christmas dinner we always had in the Mineral Lodge Coffee Shop with the Chinese cooks performing their magic. Christmas was usually a busy time for the skiers; this meant that all businesses were open before Christmas, Christmas Day, and every day after through New Year's Day. There was no time for the family as all had to work. We opened our presents on Christmas Eve because that was the only time available when we could all get together. After our family had opened presents, we usually visited our friends, Marilyn and Dick Woodward. Their parents worked for Mineral Lodge, and they had the same routine we had. Without all the fanfare associated with Christmas, we had probably the best part of Christmas. For all of my childhood and teens, I had a very white Christmas. We had frosty nights, glistening snow, icicles, and all that wonder of a snow covered landscape with the moon shining bright. The song "White Christmas" reminds me of my Christmases in Mineral every time I hear it.

CHAPTER 9

THE GIFT SHOP

The fire in January 1949, which destroyed the Lodge building, was devastating to the business and must have been demoralizing to my parents who had suffered the same disaster ten years earlier. However, it did not discourage them, as they started making plans to rebuild almost before the last ember died. This time they had good insurance coverage, and there were ample funds available. One insurance policy paid the salaries of key employees for the time the business was out of operation. One of the older cabins located directly behind the Lodge was refitted to serve as a small café during this period to accommodate the traveling public and to keep the employees working and busy.

During the month of February, my father was in San Francisco working with the Nathan Dorman Company who provided the equipment and furnishings for the new Coffee Shop. He noticed there was a wholesale gift show operating that week and had time to pay a visit there. He located one of the largest souvenir companies and ordered, sight unseen, $10,000 worth of merchandise for a gift shop in the new Mineral Lodge. He trusted the salesman to deliver to him the bestselling items for our location. Once the stuff arrived, it became my responsibility to take care of it. I do not recall if there were any words to this effect, but I knew how it was. I was just 18 then. The Gift Shop was my baby from 1949 until I sold the business in 1980.

I do not believe that the Gift Shop made any real money over those years. We did not have a good enough bookkeeping system at the time to tell which department made money. I often think how nice it would have been to have a computer then. All we had was an adding machine, a typewriter, and a telephone when it came to technology. But I do think that the Gift Shop helped the bottom line at the Lodge because it attracted people to stop and look around. It was a big draw, so no doubt worth its weight in advertising. I did my best to keep the merchandise interesting and different. This was a lot of fun.

The Gift Shop was a large building of some 60 x 30 feet. It was located in what we called the lobby with the restrooms located at the back of the room. People stopping to use the restrooms had to walk through the Gift Shop in order to get to the facilities. The restrooms were extremely basic because my father did not believe they made any money, which of course was true. But they got people to stop. If I had it to do over, I would make the restrooms quite a bit nicer; I had to clean them as part of my job. The lobby had two nice couches and four matching armchairs, plus two tables for card playing, all located in front of a large fireplace that was used for heat in the winter months.

The Gift Shop occupied a corner of this room adjacent to the front door. It consisted of six wooden cabinets with shelving on the upper portion and storage space below placed against the walls between the windows. There were also eight freestanding, wooden, flat-topped display cabinets with open shelves for storage underneath. These freestanding units could be placed in any pattern in the open space between the two walls that held the upright cabinets. Immediately to the right as you entered the door was the counter with the cash register and a glass fronted cabinet for jewelry display.

As the years went by, we built two offices in the Lodge to accommodate guest registration for the motel units and cabins,

Lobby and gift shop (Eastman Studio)

bookkeeping, and a real estate office. The real estate office occupied the original corner where the Gift Shop had started, while the guest registration office was built utilizing the opposite corner of the building. The lobby furniture disappeared and the Gift Shop took up all that space.

That first year, opening the many boxes that arrived was a real adventure. I never knew what would come out of the next box. We had to count and price every item, display some of each item on the shelves, and store the remainder where we could find it. As I remember, this took a good three weeks of my time. Edythe Englebretzen, who was the bookkeeper and also helped my mother in the Post Office, was a great help in this undertaking. She taught me the art of display. Even though she was in her late forties, she was like a kid in a candy store with each new wonder that came out of the boxes. Remember, we had not seen any of these items before and were sometimes horrified, thinking they would never sell because they were too silly and unattractive. To our amazement, we discovered that, most times, these items were the best sellers. I soon learned in my buying not to purchase what I liked, but what would sell. That first shipment consisted of a good six dozen Snookum

Indian dolls of all sizes, all with blankets as clothing. These Indian dolls did not sell very well because we were not near an Indian reservation. However, over the years they did slowly disappear. I suddenly realized that I only had six left, and they were probably, now in 1970, valuable antiques, so I took them all home. The Antique Road Show reported seeing hundreds of them each year. Recently, I attended an auction where a Snookum Indian Doll sold for $60. The dolls sold for $5.95 in the Gift Shop; however, I will not make a fortune off the ones I saved.

During all the years I managed the Gift Shop, I, and part of my family, made the annual trek to San Francisco for the Gift Show in February. It was a fun time but exhausting, walking the many aisles of the exhibition. While the Gift Shop in Mineral was more of a souvenir shop, we also sold other types of items. But I always had to remember that the souvenir junky-type of merchandise was my main bread and butter. It was lots of fun seeing all the new items each year. I first saw hookah pipes at this show. It also served as a mini vacation for me. My family had always spent time in this wonderful city and buying for the Gift Shop was good excuse for a great time in what we referred to as The City.

The Gift Shop sold salt and pepper shakers by the dozen as people collected them, and they always had to be different. We also sold lots of plaques usually printed on wood that could be hung on a wall. "You get too smart too late" is one I remember. We sold ceramic small bears, big bears, and other animals. There was also a line of animal heads to be hung on the wall—people liked these items. I sold a great amount of jewelry, mostly silver and turquoise. Rings were a big item, people loved to try them on. Usually if I spent time with the customers, they purchased a ring or two. Toward the end, I even made my own jewelry using items purchased at the gift show. I was always trying something new; some things sold well, and others did not. I once bought three dozen sweatshirts assorted by size and logos. When they arrived, I was shocked to discover that most of the shirts had rather suggestive printing on them. The one slogan I remember best said "Honk if you're horny." Needless to say these sweatshirts did not sell very well until three years later when a church group of teenagers, who had tried to climb Lassen Peak, stopped to use the restrooms. They were all freezing because they did not have proper clothing when the weather turned cold and snowy on them. The group purchased every last sweatshirt because they truly needed something warm to wear. I am not sure if the leaders even saw the logos on the shirts, but I am sure the parents did when they got home. I sold them cheerfully with a straight face, glad to be rid of them.

No matter how hard I tried, there were always items that did not sell. Sometimes they sold well one year, but when I reordered them the next, they did not move at all—and I was not always lucky with church groups as I mentioned earlier. This was a great problem until I came up with The Grab Bag. For $1 you could buy my mystery box. These were wrapped in plain, light tan paper, and you never knew what wonderful thing you might find inside—a pair of salt and pepper shakers, a wooden plaque, or who knew? In fact, this was a huge success—such a great success that I often ran out of items that did not sell and had to use real salable stuff. These $1 grab bags became a big seller over the years; people never tired of them, and I never tired of wrapping up the unwanted stuff. Sometimes the look on a ten-year-old boy's face as he unwrapped a pair of salt and pepper shakers that would have pleased his grandmother was a little heartbreaking, especially when he had taken a half-hour making his choice—but business was business.

I felt that antiques would enhance the Gift Shop; I also thought that because my mother had collected antiques that I was knowledgeable on the subject. How wrong I was! Opening that small antique shop was a real education to both Sue, my sister-in-law, and me. We fortunately started early one spring by attending antique shows in Sacramento and Williams where we purchased numerous items. We learned what they were and their value by studying books and a magazine titled *The Antique Trader*. The antiques did add to the fun of the Gift Shop, and you could shop all year for the merchandise.

I did all I could think of to promote business for Mineral Lodge. I developed art shows and flea markets in the summer months. This was easy because the nice lawn around the swimming pool was good for displaying art and setting up a booth or table for selling. People enjoyed these events, which were successful for those participating and definitely profitable for the Gift Shop and other businesses. On these occasions, the $1 Grab Bag sold out—my measure of success for the day.

After we no longer operated the Lassen Park Ski Area, we transferred the ski rentals from the Store to the Gift Shop in the winter months. This was good for the entire business of Mineral Lodge but involved a massive transferring of merchandise every spring and fall. In the fall, we packed up all the Gift Shop stuff that we could not store underneath the cabinets and trundled them by grocery cart and dolly to the small building between the Coffee Shop and the Store. Then in the spring we did the exact opposite. There was one nice aspect to these transfers: we always had lots of time, the weather was superb, and there was not a lot of business to interrupt our work. We had wonderful, leisurely lunches in the sun on the steps of the porch. It was lots of fun with good conversation. I recall these periods as the glory days. ☙

Art show at the Mineral Lodge

EDYTHE

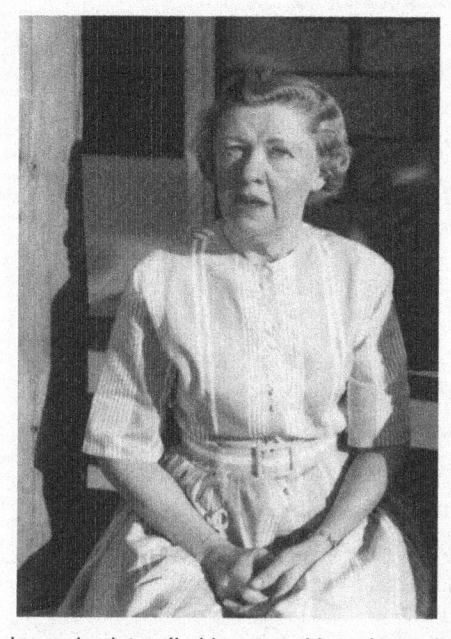

Mineral's population, which was tiny, had quite a few residents that I call "purple people." These individuals were unique. Conformity was not their cup of tea, and they liked it that way. Whether Mineral was a magnet to these people or whether they made Mineral what it was, I am not sure.

Edythe never married, by choice and circumstances. Her father owned and operated a mill in Lyonsville. She grew up there and in Red Bluff where her only sister died in an accident. Later, her father was caretaker of the Battle Creek Meadows ranch.

Edythe entered my life when she came to work for my parents sometime after the first Lodge burned down—I think I was probably nine years old. After her father's death, Edythe and her mother continued living at the ranch, and Edythe went to work for Mineral Lodge to support the two of them. She did the bookkeeping for the Lodge and helped my mother in the Post Office. Edythe brought her own lunch and always ate it on the front porch in the sun. For lunch she usually had a sandwich but always fresh carrots cut in three-quarter inch strips. Quite often, she worked late and then would have dinner with my family in the dining room. Table manners were the emphasis of these meals, and Edythe was right in there with my parents, keeping my brother, Fred, and me in line.

When her mother passed away, Edythe lived with us for a couple of months before moving into her own home in Cool Air. This is when she really took over the proper upbringing of Jo Ann. She taught me to use lemon juice as a hair rinse to keep my hair blonde. I had a bad case of pimples and black heads on my forehead that I covered with bangs. Edythe wasn't having any of that. She purchased a facial brush and scrubbed my face every night, using Skol, an alcohol-based sunscreen, as an astringent. My complexion cleared up before she moved to her home, but she made sure I continued the scrubbing routine. I owe her a lot for this. I hate to think what my teenage years would have been like with a bad complexion, as shy as I was.

Edythe loved the outdoors and took great interest in local native wild flowers and shrubs. She transplanted many of these to her yard in Mineral and took excellent care of them. One of her favorite flowers was the wild Shasta daisy. She spread its seed in the summer months as she walked to work from the Battle Creek Meadows Ranch. As a result the meadows of Mineral were covered with daisy blooms. Now sadly there are very few Shasta daisies because there is no Edythe to spread their seed. She liked to be outdoors as often as she could, so she insisted that her day off be a day with good weather. This was difficult to accomplish sometimes, but we all did our best to accommodate her.

Edythe loved cowboys and horses as she had spent her youth in this environment. She was welcome at the McKenzie ranch to help with the cattle, and she did this often. Like the cowboys, she liked her whiskey, and not an evening went by that she didn't have an alcoholic beverage of some type. She was no alcoholic, she just liked her booze. She turned down a good marriage proposal, I believe, because the man was a teetotaler, and he was not a cowboy. Often, when we had finished work, Edythe would invite my sister-in-law, Sue, and me to have drinks with her before we went home to cook dinner for our families. She liked sherry wine and poured a small, cheese-glass full. There were times I wondered how I got dinner on the table because of the powerful effects of the sherry.

Edythe's bookkeeping job was in the same building as the Gift Shop, so she was there advising me in every step of the operation. She was especially good at displaying the merchandise. It was her idea to move things to different locations to make it look like new items had arrived. I believe today I am a fair interior decorator because we constantly changed the location of the souvenirs and gifts, and I developed an eye for what looks best.

When my mother retired from the Post Office, Edythe took her place. My mother never read a postcard when she was in that position. Apparently, Edythe did, and I could not blame her—it was a boring job. At a family Thanksgiving dinner a few years after Edythe's death, Sue's mother mentioned something about some correspondence to Fred from a lady of the night in Nevada. We were all confused until Elizabeth said that Edythe had told her about it. Then we remembered that on our trip across country, my husband, George, and I had stopped in Nevada and sent such a postcard to Fred as a joke. Poor Edythe must have worried about this for years.

In her late sixties, Edythe developed breast cancer. She had the lump removed but refused to go to San Francisco for any further treatment even though she had good friends in the city who would have taken care of her. She just could not see herself away from Mineral in a strange place. The cancer returned, and she treated it with every folk remedy she knew. She would not let me or anyone else help her with anything. I can still see her in this old blue bathrobe, piped in white, telling us she was fine. She had a closet full of very fancy bathrobes given to her by friends, but she would not wear any of them. She did admit herself into the Chester hospital "to get some rest." She, of course, did not return and is not buried in Lyonsville, as she wanted, but in Red Bluff. I take Dogwood every spring and fall to my family's plot and also to Edythe's grave—the white flowers in the spring and the red leaves in the fall. I feel I was very fortunate to have had her in my life, and I always include fresh carrots whenever I take a packed lunch.

Mineral Lodge Buffet, c. 1935 (Eastman Studio)

The buffet, c. 1968 (left to right, Jo Ann Perkins, chef, and George Perkins)

CHAPTER 10

THE BUFFET

The Buffet was used in the first Mineral Lodge in 1935 to designate what we would call the Bar today. I am not sure why they used the term Buffet, maybe to distinguish it from a saloon or maybe the term "bar" as we know it today wasn't in vogue. The Buffet was at the north end of the building. It had a long, high bar with stools and several mounted black-tailed deer heads around the walls. It was not adjacent to the Coffee Shop, which makes me think they did not serve any drinks in the eating establishment then. However, the next Mineral Lodge, built in 1940, used the same name, Buffet, but it was next to the restaurant for the convenience of serving alcohol.

My mother told me that when Prohibition ended in 1931, my father said, "I believe I should obtain the license for selling liquor because it will be good for business." My father was, however, familiar with liquor; my mother often told the story of one of her first dates with my father during Prohibition. She came from a farming community that never touched liquor. She taught in the local high school, and she always obeyed the law. It seems they left Corning for Red Bluff on a rainy night. Halfway there my father turned off the highway onto a dirt road and proceeded to stop in the middle of a field. He got out, opened a trap door, and retrieved a few bottles of bootleg booze to take to his friend, Mickey Hornbeck, in Red Bluff. My mother was severely shaken by her first experience of rum-running.

So Mineral Lodge has always had two liquor licenses: off-sale and on-sale. The off-sale license was used in the grocery store for bottled liquor, wine, and beer; the on-sale was used for the bar. There was, and still is, also two different types of licenses for on-sale liquor depending on whether you sold food or not. The on-sale licenses that do not sell food are not allowed to have minors under the age of 21 on the premises. Any age person has always been allowed in the Mineral Lodge Buffet or bar.

The Bar in the present Lodge built in 1949 is not called either a bar or Buffet, but simply The Rafter Room. Don Clever, who had designed the Palomino Room in Red Bluff, was responsible for this clever design, and it does have rafters which are 4 x 4 inch beams, crisscrossing the ceiling. There is nothing square in the room; the bar sits at an angle, as do the rafters. The most unique features of the room are the windows made of old, colored beer bottles set in concrete and backed by heavy glass on either side of the window. These bottles came from an old brewery in Red Bluff and are brown, green, or white. There is also a backbar that originally had a beautiful, square, stone, open fireplace in the middle of the room. It has the same rafters.

In the name of money and entertainment, the fireplace was removed to make room for a pool table and pinball machines. My older daughter, Heidi, can beat most people at pool because one summer she broke both of her wrists falling off a horse. She was 13 at the time and could not swim or do much else with the two casts on. She learned to play pool with these stiff wrists to entertain herself.

The Rafter Room was usually a social hall where vacationers, summer homeowners, and locals gathered. There was no age restriction, so children of all ages were welcome with their parents. When NASA landed on the moon in 1969, The Rafter Room had

The Rafter Room with George Perkins (Eastman Studio)

one of the few televisions in Mineral. Everyone packed the room to view the fuzzy black and white images of the astronauts walking on the moon.

My husband, George, was responsible for managing The Rafter Room. His first task on moving to Mineral involved the sales tax paid to the State of California for all taxable sales generated by Mineral Lodge. Sales tax is paid to the state by the owner of a bar, even though a customer does not pay it as you do with other taxable items. The bar owner just absorbs the cost. The State can and does audit businesses if they think the business is not paying the proper amount. In this instance, the State had audited the bar books and, based on liquor purchased from the liquor wholesaler, demanded another $3,000 in sales tax. George was a Second Lieutenant in the Army during the Korean War; his job was to supervise Army auditors in the Midwest. He also had a business degree from the University of Colorado. It took him a day or two to discover an error in the State's calculations. Not only did we not owe them money, they owed us.

The fallout from this incident lasted until I sold the business in 1980. My father, Husky, did not like book work as he felt he was doing work for the government, so his books were subject to many government audits. Husky thought this was great because the auditor had to stay at Mineral Lodge and eat in the restaurant. I am sure the auditors did not like the job because Husky's office was in an unheated building and wasn't too organized. Husky paid the bills when he had money and put all paid invoices on two-hole punch boards. When the boards filled up, he removed the invoices from the boards and tied them up with rawhide lacing. These stacks of invoices were stored in boxes in an attic space over the office, reached by a folding stairway. The attic area had open air vents at either end of the small building that pulled in small bits of ash from an open incinerator behind the building. So the auditor had to search for the necessary papers with ash floating around. Between George's re-audit and Husky's office practices, we never had another audit or question of our government reports.

We had many bartenders over the years. Leonard Irish was the bartender for many years, as was Bob Smith. They were gregarious, likeable people, and, above all, were honest. But others were not so honest. It is difficult for the owner to control costs if the bartender gives away free drinks or pockets some of the money instead of putting it in the cash register. One particular individual took the prize for his dishonesty. He did not give away free drinks. Rather he just took full liquor bottles home with him, and he did this in daylight right under our noses so to speak. He played his guitar and sang to the guests. Everyone loved to hear him, and the bar traffic increased while he was working. He only worked for a couple of months one summer, and then he was gone. When I added up the wholesale liquor costs for the one month after he left, I discovered a large discrepancy between the sales and the costs—the costs being much higher for the amount of sales registered. It seems he had brought his guitar case in every day with his guitar in it. When he went home, his guitar case was also full of liquor bottles. What he did with the liquor we never found out.

Bernie Gleason was one of the best bartenders we had. He was good at telling stories, and he had a knack for timing. He never finished his story when customers who were listening had an empty glass. They usually had to buy another drink to hear the end of the story. The bar sales increased when he was on duty. But there is a very funny story about Bernie himself. He grew up on the south side of Chicago ending up in Red Bluff via Aberdeen, Washington, where he taught in the local high school. He only tended bar in the summer months as he had a summer cabin in Mill Creek. One winter in Red Bluff, his next-door neighbor told Bernie that he had called the local police because he had a rabid dog in his yard. The next week or so Bernie saw a chicken in his yard. Coming from Chicago, he thought the chicken was probably rabid, so he called the local police who came and removed the chicken. He did not think anything about it until the following week when he heard all the people laughing about the man who called the police to remove the chicken from his yard. Bernie had such a good sense of humor that he told the story on himself, but he never called the police again for a chicken. On this same subject of chickens—I had a roommate in college who grew up in San Francisco, whose sister asked if a chicken had three legs. The answer was yes.

We had many customers over the years, and the bar attracted entertaining and unusual people, as well as the sad and lonely. We had many unhappy people who needed someone to tell their troubles to. One of the most entertaining that I recall were forest firefighters from one of the government agencies. They had beautiful tenor voices and loved to sing. They would pop in, have a drink, sing a few songs, and be gone. We also had many people who came year after year to stay in Mineral for their vacation. A man I will call Skipper Bob was one of our perpetual customers in the bar. His story is not typical of Mineral but shows how unusual things can take place.

Skipper Bob started coming to Mineral Lodge sometime around 1960. He was a bartender in San Francisco and usually came in the fall of the year for the deer hunting season. His attire consisted of a fringed buckskin jacket with a brace of bullets diagonally over each shoulder, the mark of a true hunter! There were stories that he did not hunt but came for the recreation of the Mineral Bar, and this was probably true. He was around six feet tall and weighed a good 225 pounds and always had three-day stubble on his face. He did not seem to have any family as far as we knew. George worked all day one day to give each of the bartenders a day off. One particular fall, the regular bartender's mother died, and George had to tend bar everyday for over two weeks. Skipper Bob showed up about this time, so George had a good dose of him night after night. When Skipper Bob wanted another drink, he would say, "Give me a little smile." He always stayed until closing time at 2:00 a.m., so George would come home a mental basket case after his long, boring hours with Skipper Bob.

Over the years, as Skipper Bob grew older, we all developed a certain fondness toward him. He started bringing a friend along, named Captain Jack. They would rent a housekeeping cabin, and Skipper Bob would not spend all of his time in the bar. He developed heart trouble, his hair thinned and grayed, and his ankles swelled. He did not look well, and it was painful for him to walk. Bob had not been to Mineral for two years, and we thought he had passed away, when he surprised us by making a reservation for a week's stay. My brother, Fred, and George were looking forward to seeing him. I was working at the Gift Shop cash register when I heard George shouting to Fred who was working on the baseball field across the highway, "Fred, Skipper Bob is here sitting in the car looking like he is dead." His voice changed "Maybe he is dead." George looked closer in the car and saw that the man was not moving. Fred ran across the highway and on closer inspection they determined that Skipper Bob was not alive.

It did not take the two men long to find Captain Jack in the Bar having a great time. When questioned about Skipper Bob, he reported that they had eaten lunch in Vacaville, but when they stopped for the usual drink at the Green Barn in Red Bluff, Skipper Bob did not get out of the car. Captain Jack had his usual drink alone and continued on to Mineral where he left Skipper Bob in the car where George found him. He apparently did not notice anything unusual.

I called the county coroner, and he requested that we move the car to the shade until he arrived as it was a hot day. Ed Pine, the local telephone repairman, offered to move the car as neither Fred nor George was anxious for the job. Ed was not as excited about the job when Skipper Bob's body fell over toward him as he backed the car up. However, he recovered his composure by joining Fred, George, Captain Jack, and many others in the bar. This was a Sunday in the summer with lots of people around, and the incident had unnerved everyone. Captain Jack came into the Gift Shop and asked me to help him make a telephone call to the San Francisco bar where Skipper Bob had worked all of his life. His report was "Yes, deader than a door nail." He told me that the patrons of the San Francisco bar had all bet on how long Skipper Bob would live.

When the coroner arrived, he was a little suspicious that there had been some foul play because most of the witnesses were in the bar drinking. I assured him that this was not the case, it was just a typical Sunday afternoon in the Mineral Bar. This was not quite the truth, but it satisfied him.

Owning and operating a bar is different to say the least. You never knew who might come through the door, especially after 11:00 p.m. Most people were ordinary, but occasionally a real weirdo would arrive. We treated them with kindness and hoped they would be on their way soon. These late night stragglers were usually on their way to Reno and did not stay long. My friend Barbara Jackson has written a small piece concerning an incident she witnessed which truly imparts these situations, and she has allowed me to include it here:

In the early 1990s the Mineral bar continued to be a gathering place as it had been for many years. The following is a look at one story of many gatherings at the bar.

One stormy, rainy night a gust of wind blew into the Mineral bar room as the heavy wooden door was slowly pushed opened. We all watched to see who was going to come dragging through the door. The door opened a few inches at a time and a huge plastic hat poked through the opening. As the door opened a little wider, a crutch immerged then a second crutch. Finally a very large man, extremely bent over, looking very worn and wet, squeezed through the door, one leg at a time. Right behind him a woman pushed her way in as well. She looked younger than the man, but just as worn and very wet. From her mouth hung a lit cigarette from which she took a puff as she asked Ron, the bartender, if they could warm up by the fire.

Ron replied, "Help yourself." The man shuffled to the back of the room where the wood stove was emitting a warm glow of heat. Puppet Master 2 was playing on the TV in the bar room, and had most of our attention. It was just getting to the really scary parts. The movie told the story of puppets who come to life at the command of a man who is living on the fluid of other people. Scary.

The woman walked to the back room where the wood stove was located and sat down with the man to try to dry out. I thought they must be cold and wet, so I suggested that Ron might give them a cup of coffee. Someone mentioned that these were the two folks standing in the rain all afternoon, hitchhiking on the highway, not far from the bar. There was much discussion about whether it was okay to hitchhike in Mineral or not. No one really came up with a legitimate answer.

The woman sauntered back toward the bar and asked if many cars passed through Mineral during the night. Everyone said, "No" all at once. I saw this worried her greatly. She then looked out the door to see if their packs were still outside under the overhanging part of the roof, safe from the rain. Ron poured them cups of steaming hot coffee and she sat down at the bar. I asked her where they were coming from and she answered, "San Diego, El Cajon to be exact." She explained that she had been looking for her daughter there. Her daughter was married to a Navy man and she had not seen the daughter in two years. The man and the woman were now headed for Susanville, then on to Idaho where the woman's brother lived. She bent over slowly, picked up the two cups of coffee, and walk toward the man in the back room. She tried to talk the man into coming to the front of the room where the bar is.

After a while he shuffled out to check their stuff. He asked Ron if he could bring it inside. Ron says, "Okay," and the man limped slowly out the door and began dragging huge soaking wet packs into the room. He proceeded to stash them under the shuffle board table. I went outside and helped him with the door since the wind was howling and the rain was coming down harder than ever. He then dragged himself over to the bar, took out all of his change, dropped it on the bar, and asked, "Is this enough for another cup of coffee?" Ron said, "You get a free refill." The man scratched at the money with huge rough fingers, apparently unable to pick up the money because he has no finger nails. Somehow he managed to pick up the loose change off the bar. He then returned to the back room with his coffee to again warm himself by the fire. A few minutes later he came back to the bar and asked Ron in a tone that is barely understandable, "Is there a preacher in this town?" Ron said "No." We all came to the conclusion that he was trying to figure out where to stay for the night. He then returned to the back room and joined the lady waiting to see what he had learned.

We all took a moment from our scary movie to think of somewhere the two unfortunate people could stay for the night. We decided that the post office would be the best place since there was no church in Mineral, and the post office is the only place open all night where they could stay warm and dry.

Ron was elected to tell them they could stay by the fire until closing, but they must then make a short walk up the highway to the post office. The man and woman decided that they would make the journey up the highway now, before closing. They picked up their heavy sodden bags and pushed their way out the door. The door banged behind them.

There was a lot of chatter in the bar after they left, about what would happen to them and why did someone not take them in, but no one volunteered. We all continued watching Puppets Master 2 on the bar TV and wondered: What would happen to this interesting couple who wandered into the Mineral bar on that stormy night. It would be a story told over and over again for many years. For Mineral this was an exciting evening at the Mineral Bar.

I myself had a situation where I was relieved to see someone come through the bar door. It concerned Lassen West, an attempt to shift some skiers to the small hill west of the Lodge. We had formed a group, raised money, and constructed a small rope tow, but we could not start operations until it was inspected and approved by the state. The inspector called one day in advance to say when he would be there. It was a busy weekend, and all of the motels and cabins were full, and he needed a place to spend the night. My children were all in Tahoe, so I gladly offered him this accommodation. Not a bad idea until it became apparent that he was looking forward to more than a place to sleep. So at about 11:00 p.m. there was me, Chuck Kindig the bartender, the inspector, and a young couple playing shuffle board. The young couple left, and then there were the three of us. I was not about to take this man home, but I did not know quite how to solve the problem. Guess what? The bar door opened, and in came the young couple with a local lady whose husband had died the year before. They had encountered her on their walk home through Cool Air, the subdivision just across the street from the lodge. The inspector and the lady were enchanted with each other, and they all left within half an hour. Chuck closed the bar immediately, and after I was sure there was no one watching, I went home, locked the doors, and turned out the lights.

Lassen West's rope tow passed inspection without a problem the next day. Lassen West was my idea, a great name but a bad idea. The south-facing hill in those years did not get enough snow, and we were only able to operate it a few days.

BETTY BROWN

Betty was old enough to be my mother, but because of her youthful attitude it never seemed to make a difference. Betty grew up in Marin County, where her family owned The Schmidt Lithograph Company in San Francisco. She and her best friend, Jean, came to ski at Mineral one winter. There the two of them met two gentlemen, Harvey Brown and Sadie Lilenthal, who came from Westwood. The men worked in the lumber industry but were wintering in Mineral for the skiing, living in one of the small cabins on the Mineral Lodge property. Betty fell in love with Harvey and Jean with Sadie. Both couples later married.

Harvey and Betty built a lovely house in Cool Air and had two children, Rick and Robin. They were living in Mineral operating the Mineral Mill when my husband, George, and I moved there in 1956. Harvey was an avid skier, and we all became good friends. Unfortunately, Harvey died of cancer a few years later, and Betty came to work for the Mineral Lodge as a bookkeeper. She also worked on weekends at the Ski Area selling lift tickets, coffee, and hamburgers. The bathroom facilities were pit toilets located in the parking lot and required walking outside in inclement weather. Betty's claim to fame was that she never had to use them during the day.

Betty was an excellent employee. She did all the work necessary to keep the back-office going and also helped with the Gift Shop and motel registration. Her home was our real party place; she was always eager for fun and loved having people around. If you needed to talk about some problem, she was always available. She designed the house herself with a great stone fireplace that always had a warm, welcoming fire. When stereo first came out, Betty sent for, and built, her own system. She had a large collection of Life magazines that she had saved over the years.

My first big trip was taken with Betty in 1965. We visited Egypt, Lebanon, Israel, Greece, and Jordan. What adventures we had seeing those countries. In Luxor, Egypt, we stayed in a grand old hotel that I have forgotten the name of. As we snuggled in our beds for the night, we both noticed a nice sized hole in the mattresses for our back sides. I will never forget Betty's remark, "I wonder how many fannies have slept in this bed." From the size of the indentation, a good many people had been there before us.

Betty and I also traveled for six weeks in Europe with my sister-in-law, Sue, and Betty Bauer who had worked with us at the Ski Hut. We traveled on the trains and slept in bed-and-breakfasts. We never required a tour guide as we used *Europe on $5 a Day* by Eric Frommer. We visited most of central Europe and Scandinavia, even going to Berlin through then-occupied East Germany. Our costs turned out to be slightly higher—$8 a day. But compared to today's prices, we had a real bargain. Betty took it upon herself to decide when we should be at the station for our next train trip. As the time grew closer to going home, Betty kept having us wait longer and longer for the train. I remember waiting for over an hour in Sweden, freezing, with no place to sit. She also kept telling us when the Mineral Bar was closing according to the local time where we were.

Betty eventually worked for the Park Service in Mineral, later retiring to Grass Valley where she designed and built another beautiful home. After a few years, she built an additional home in Mineral, spending most of her summers there. Her descendants still enjoy this home, keeping touch with their deep roots in Mineral.

CHAPTER 11

CABINS

Battle Creek Meadows, or Hamptons, was the first designated name for Mineral. When my grandfather and Warren Woodson purchased the property in 1920, they changed the name to Mineral Camp Site, which evolved over the years to Mineral Lodge and/or Lassen Mineral Lodge.

At one time, there were 23 cabins and 10 or 12 tent rentals. The tent rentals had wooden sides of rough lumber with a tent roof. These tent cabins were gone by 1935, and there were 14 cabins available for rent. The remaining nine cabins still existed, but were not in suitable condition to be rented and were used for employee housing. The 15-acre area encompassing these cabins was east of the Lodge with dirt roads connecting them. The cabins were small, 500 square feet, with two bedrooms, one bath, combined living room-kitchen, and a front porch. The 14 cabins enjoyed a high occupancy during the 1940s and 1950s from the middle of June until October 15 when the deer hunting season ended. During the summer months, they were occupied mostly by families of French and Italian descent from San Francisco and deer hunters after that. I remember that most of the older people in the summer months did not speak English, but they came year after year and always rented the same cabin. My father had a unique method for handling the reservations: he used plywood boards, usually 4 x 2 feet, covered with butcher paper with the cabin numbers down the left side and the weeks across the top. This left a square space for each cabin for each week. You can imagine how inconvenient it was when you had a reservation request on the telephone and had to balance this board while writing the information down in the correct square. I can't remember that any of us ever complained, and we never had a mistake or a mix-up on a reservation.

After WWII, my father built six housekeeping cabins that were larger, 900 square feet, with the same basic design. These were very popular with both new and old customers. But as families became larger with the baby boom, all of our cabins were woefully too small—and not only too small, they were old. People expected and demanded more luxurious accommodations. Not only were the cabins too small and too old, the upkeep on them was horrendous. Toilets were always malfunctioning, the cabins needed painting inside and out and were dusty in the summer, and the dirt roads needed maintenance. We oiled the roads at the beginning of every summer to keep the dust down, but this was really a bad solution. People complained, and the vacancy factor increased every year. It was a losing situation.

One of the problems with the cabins was the employees needed to maintain them. Mineral was such a small community that we could not usually find suitable people willing or capable to work for us. We usually hired people through the state employment agency in Red Bluff. It seemed a good idea to hire a couple, the man to do the maintenance and the wife to do the changing of the beds and cleaning. This usually did not work very well, because if the man worked hard and was good at his job, the wife was the opposite—lazy and difficult for us to keep her working. If the woman was perfect for the job, the husband was only so–so. But we kept hiring couples until one man's wife died from a heart condition, and we hired a separate lady for the housekeeping. This worked well for a few years, although I did discover after he left that the man never fixed anything too well—just enough to make sure we always needed him to fix it again. We had many different men over the years; one particularly nice, older gentleman from Corning had been there only a few weeks when I discovered quite a few red rags in the back of the pickup he used to haul garbage. I suddenly remembered that I had stored a case of sterno cans used for the summer buffet in a cabin he had access to. I had read that alcoholics used the sterno by soaking the rags and squeezing out the fumes for a high. This man went back to Corning in a hurry, and I kept the sterno in a safer location.

My husband, George, and I often attended ski movies. While watching one in Chico, we were shocked and surprised to see one of our newer housekeeping cabins on the screen. The movie showed the good things about skiing and the adverse. Our cabin was featured as an unpleasant accommodation for skiers. We had a good laugh about it, but it did bring up the fact that we were way behind the times. So, in 1965, we borrowed $25,000 to upgrade all 20 housekeeping cabins with new paint, and new, larger decks. This helped some, but the problems still existed—they were still out of style, and it was painful to try and rent them to people from the

Cabins and the areas behind them that were logged in the early 1940s (Eastman Studio)

city. Mineral just did not have that great an appeal to overcome the poor housekeeping accommodations.

We were at our wit's end with the cabin problem until I came up with the brilliant idea to subdivide the cabin area and sell those monsters. It took George a good year to execute the plan by creating a subdivision that we called Lassen Alpine Village. We had to tear down the existing cabins that were not salable. This we accomplished by advertising free lumber from these structures if you demolished them yourself and carried off the lumber. We had no trouble finding people willing and eager to do this. The salable cabins needed new hot water heaters and the existing wiring upgraded to current code. The roads in the area had to be paved and improved up to Tehama County standards. Along with the 20 cabins in this new subdivision, we had an additional 15 lots to sell. Depending on the size, we sold the cabins for $4,500 to $9,500. The vacant lots sold for $3,000 to $5,000 depending on size and location. Cabins or lots could be purchased for 10% down with the balance due in five or ten years. We held the notes on these purchases and charged the current interest rate. We turned an

Mineral cabins looking south toward Turner Mountain (photograph by H.C. Linn)

Mineral cabins (Eastman Studio)

albatross into a big asset, and everybody, including our customers, was happy as a clam.

Several people who had been customers over the years bought their favorite cabins; one family still owns that cabin today. People who purchased their cabins only used the cabin for two or three weeks a year, thus making the cabin available for the balance of the year. I obtained a California Real Estate License and, as a property manager, rented the cabins to the public at the going rate. This was again a win-win for all concerned. I used the money to take a special trip every year, and the owners were happy with the extra income. Originally I started with eight or nine cabins to rent, but this had dwindled down to only two or three by the time I sold the lodge in 1980.

Merrill Woodward and bear kill at the garage, c. 1934
(courtesy Floy Woodward)

CHAPTER 12

GARAGE AND SERVICE STATION

We had Merrill Woodward in the Store, and we had Paul Becker in the Garage. Paul grew up in Corning, and when he came to Mineral I am not sure. He had always been there as long as I can remember. He was a wonderful mechanic; he could fix anything. People brought their cars from Red Bluff and Corning for him to repair. There were always cars waiting for his magic touch. The working area in the garage did not look organized, but Paul knew where every wrench or tool he needed was because he could remember where he had used it last. He served in the Merchant Marines during World War II. My father took over Paul's duties, except fixing cars, while he was gone. The two motels were heated by boilers. Paul knew how to maintain and fix these monsters as well.

Paul mostly lived alone and ate all of his meals in the Coffee Shop. He would work late into the night if the job required it. He was always eating dinner as we were cleaning up for the night. It seemed during the summer months he worked mostly day and night. I remember his belt always fit him snugly in June, but by September he had a good five inches of extra leather because he lost weight due to his long hours of hard work.

I am not sure when the service station or garage was built. Early pictures show the beginnings of the service station in the 1920s. The garage was no doubt erected in the 1930s. As a form of advertising, the roof of the garage, which faced west, had a finger pointing across the street to the Lodge proper. The finger was painted white with a green background. It was very effective as you could see it a good half-mile away.

Rock McClellen tells the story that his father painted the sign. As he was painting, my father, Husky, told him it was out of proportion, and he would not be able to finish it correctly. Well, Husky was wrong. The painter knew his business. The sign looked great and stayed there for years. It was only replaced when the roof fell in from heavy snow in 1970.

Standard Oil had loaned my father the money to build the station in order to ensure that their Chevron brand of gasoline was the only gas sold. Standard was easy to deal with, and the loan was amortized over the years. The year before the roof of the garage collapsed, all insurance companies had cancelled coverage of snow damage because they had suffered great losses in the Tahoe area from heavy snows that year. It was a tough break for Mineral Lodge because we never had extra money, plus we had paid high insurance premiums over the years to insure ourselves against such a catastrophic event. Again, Standard Oil gave us a new loan and assistance in designing the new building.

As I said before, Paul could fix anything. One of the best examples I can remember was in 1957. We obtained a ten-year lease for Lassen Park Ski Area that fall and installed a new Poma lift on the mountain to carry skiers up the hill. On our second day of operation, which was early January due to the late arrival of snow, the cable fell off both bull wheels on the lift and was lying on top of the snow. I remember how shocked I was. I thought things just ran; it had never occurred to me that something might break down. Well, the cable never fell off the bull wheels again after Paul remembered an old automobile part lying around in the woods. He retrieved the part, reconstructed it, and installed it on the lift, fixing the situation permanently.

Paul's favorite recreation was playing Keno in Reno. He always played the same numbers, and he always played in the same clubs. He would spend a day or two just walking between the different Keno games. He had it timed to get to all his favorite places. Over the years, he won one or two jackpots of $12,500 and several smaller ones. I remember one particularly cold November when there was very little business in Mineral and my sister-in-law, Sue, and I were in charge of the whole operation in Mineral because our husbands were in the Bay Area selling Christmas Trees. As we relied on Paul to help us with any mechanical problems, we were surprised to find he had gone to Reno. He returned in two days relating to us that he had won $3,500. All I could think about was that I should have gone to Reno and followed Paul instead of sitting in Mineral. ✌

Garage and service station (Eastman Studio)

Mineral Lodge pool. The area in the background became Cool Air II and Meadow View II

Golf course that became the Meadow View Subdivision

CHAPTER 13

THE SUBDIVISIONS

Mineral would not be what it is today if it were not for the work done to subdivide the land into lots for people to build cabins on. The very first tract was done by the grandmaster himself, Warren Woodson. Remember, he was the one who developed the town of Corning. He and my grandfather purchased the land in Mineral in 1920. My grandfather died shortly thereafter, but that did not stop Woodson. He had developed a 120-lot subdivision called Cool Air by 1928. This is the area directly across Hwy 36 from the Mineral Lodge. The size of each lot was 50 x 100 feet. Water was provided directly to the lot, and a sanitary sewer system was also available. The sewer system consisted of leach fields in the south part of present-day Scenic Avenue. No doubt not good by modern standards but state of art in the 1920s. These lots, depending on their location, sold for $200 to $300. You could also purchase a lot for a small down payment and pay off the balance with monthly payments. The majority of the lots were purchased by families from Corning and Red Bluff. This was before air conditioning, and people needed to get out of that summer heat. Mineral was a close-by escape. Martha Slade from Corning told me her family had built their cabin in Cool Air in 1930 for $250. The Maywood Hotel in Corning, also owned by Woodson, had a large photograph of Mineral Lodge hanging in the lobby, with the caption "90 MINUTES IN HIGH GEAR TO MINERAL." This picture now hangs in the Mineral Lodge restaurant.

By 1929, the Forest Service had subdivided 60 lots for people to lease. These lots were 90 x 175 feet. The original leases ran 99 years for $15 a year. These lots also were furnished with a water system, but sewage disposal was up to the homeowner. Originally, sewage disposal consisted of a hole filled with rocks called a cesspool; later septic tanks were required and still are. The official name for this area was Home Owners, but was commonly referred to by locals as String Town. In the early 1950s, another 48 lots were made available. The original leases for 99 years were later changed to one year. In 1970, the lessees were able to obtain similar land in another area of the state and trade the new parcel to the government for their original lots. This gave them fee simple title to the land and greatly increased the value of their cabins.

My father, Husky, built the next subdivision in 1950 with 25 lots along the hillside west of the Lodge. I was given the privilege of naming the area Meadow View. These lots were somewhat larger than the original ones in Cool Air. Again, water was provided to the lots, but the homeowners had to provide their own septic tanks for sewage.

Husky gave up his golf course for this tract. The golf course had five holes on the north side of Hwy 36, the remaining four on the south side. Hole #1 in the course required the golfer to drive his ball up the hill that sits next to the Lodge; hole #2 was down the hill. Husky even had a mower to keep the grass cut on the course. When he closed the course, he gave the mower to his next favorite place to play golf, that being the Wilcox Club in Red Bluff. Husky was one of backers for that club when it first became public.

I married George in 1955, and we moved to Mineral the next year to assist in the management of the Lassen Park Ski Area. George had grown up on the North Shore of Chicago, had a business degree from the University of Colorado, and had led an audit team

Frank McCaughey's mother at Cool Air, c. 1931
(McCaughey family collection)

for the U.S. Army. Mineral was a great shock to him as he was a jolt for Mineral. George felt Mineral was a very difficult place to make money, and it was! Subsequently, in his search for additional sources of income, he decided we needed to subdivide more land. In the ensuing years, he did just that. He developed 28 lots in Meadow View II on the remaining land of the old golf course. We had used this land as a driving range, renting the balls from the Gift Shop. George developed Cool Air II on the land that was the original sewer system for Cool Air I with 42 lots. He also built a tennis court in conjunction with these lots, tennis being his favorite sport next to skiing. He subdivided the Mineral Lodge cabin area, calling it Lassen Alpine Village, with a total of 56 lots with or without cabins. The lots with smaller cabins sold for $4,000 and the larger cabins for $9,000. Again we sold a cabin or a lot for a small down payment and monthly payments including interest. Obtaining final approval for a subdivision from the California State Department of Subdivisions is complicated and time consuming, and George personally did all the work for these three subdivisions. Meadow

View II was the easiest with a file folder about an inch thick; by the time he had approval for Lassen Alpine Village, the file was over three inches thick. We all shared in the profits, but George did all the work.

This is no doubt the end of my story of Mineral subdivisions for now. There is land available, but it is not zoned for subdivisions because the State of California years ago rezoned all land with growing trees as Timber Preserve. The zoning of Timber Preserve is similar to Agriculture Preserve. The owner must petition to have the zoning changed in ten years time.

CHAPTER 14

THE MINERAL SCHOOL

I have had a long and somewhat adventurous life. I am proud of what I have accomplished and the places I have been. But I am the proudest and look back with the fondest of memories to my eight years in the Mineral School. I was the first person to go through all eight grades and graduate from this school. At the time, this accomplishment did not thrill me because I had to face entering Red Bluff High School with a student body of 500; Mineral Elementary student body was 18. This was a quantum leap for a shy, introverted little girl of 14.

Mineral had a one-room school when I entered the first grade in 1937. My mother had looked ahead and started working to establish a school district in Mineral soon after I was born in 1931. The district was finally a reality in 1934, and she served on the school board for many years. She told me that it had been quite a struggle because the new Mineral district took away territory from the Oak Park and Pine Grove School districts, and they did not like losing the tax base. In 1937, the school had maybe 10 students. When I graduated eight years later, the student body had doubled.

The three lots for the school were donated by my parents and Warren Woodson. The first building stood where the playground

Mineral School, c. 1965 (courtesy Joel Rienhard)

Mineral Students, c. 1939. Jo Ann Beresford, 2nd row, 3rd from right.

is today. The building was approximately 20 x 50 feet with a 12 x 20 foot covered porch. My mother donated the large bell that hung above the porch. This bell originally came from Hampton's store. I started school every morning with the ringing of that bell and every call to class for the remainder of the day. It had a great resounding tone, and I can still hear it. In the middle of the porch the front door led to a small hall with bathrooms on either side. The remainder of the building was the classroom with a wood or oil heater in the center of the room for heat. Each side of the room had windows. Along the front of the building, backing the restrooms, were wooden lockers and storage shelves. The back of the building led to an earth-floor woodshed.

We began each school day by reciting the Pledge of Allegiance and singing "America" or "America the Beautiful." We started the pledge with our hand over our heart until we reached the words "to the flag" at which time we pointed to the flag and extended our arm full length. Sometime during World War II we stopped extending our arm because it resembled the Nazi "Heil Hitler" salute. At 10:00 a.m., we had a short 10-minute recess followed by class until 11:00 a.m. when we had Physical Education. The teacher organized outdoor play for 20 minutes. The games I remember were kickball, work up baseball, and capture the flag. Lunch time was noon. Some students went home for lunch, and the rest ate home-packed lunches at their desks. There was free play after you finished lunch. Class resumed at 1:00 p.m. until 2:00 p.m. when the older grades had another 10-minute recess and the lower grades, one through three, were released for the day. The remaining grades stayed until 3:30 p.m. As I remember, we mostly played outside even in inclement weather; everyone was well equipped and dressed for rain or snow. One winter when we had a lot of snow, we built a snow fort with a covered roof that was lots of fun.

One memory about my time in the Mineral School is that there were no traumas. There were so few of us that everyone got along and cooperated with the teacher and other students. I do not remember teaching others or older students teaching me, which is said to have been the norm in many one-room schools. All I can say is that my education was good enough for me to graduate from high school and the university. The one exception was phonics, which must have escaped me somehow; I do not pronounce unfamiliar words easily. But I do remember teachers reading aloud from nonfiction stories about Alaska and the far north as we huddled around the stove to keep warm. I remember trying to listen by radio to the Standard Symphonic Hour that was broadcast for schools such as ours. Radio reception was not good in Mineral, and we could only hear parts of the broadcast here and there.

Another memory is a project we had concerning South America when I was assigned to research Columbia. This project opened up the world beyond Mineral to me, and I have tried to visit as many places around the globe as I can since. I remember standing in the small entry of the school wondering about outer space and if someday people would be able to fly to the moon. I also had one teacher who had lived in Malaysia for several years. She taught us many things from the cultures of the Indian, Chinese, and Malay. She even wrote a play for us to perform featuring the differences. I still know how to put on an Indian sari.

My teacher in the first grade was Mrs. McMann who was related to the Kellys of the Kelly-Griggs House Museum in Red Bluff. The teacher in 1934 was Nancy Turner who brought her three children with her in order to bring the student body up to five so that school could commence. There were many teachers over the years; some taught for many years while many stayed only one year. Thelma Moore taught in the early years. Ethel Warren taught from 1947 through 1956, Gabrielle Brown from 1960 to 1977, and Jane Hoofard taught from 1987 to 2000.

There are some interesting stories concerning the teachers who only lasted one year. One gentleman, who had sailed his own boat around the world, established a yearly school trip after he discovered that one of his students had not been east of Westwood, west of Red Bluff, north beyond Redding, or south of Corning.

He wanted his students to see more of the world. These trips were taken to different cities over several years. Another single gentleman was invited to dinner by the Hallocks, but showed up at the Hafleys who fed him without a word. He only learned of his mistake the next day when the Hallocks asked why he had not come for dinner.

Mineral remained a one-room school town until around 1947 when a second building was constructed for use as a gymnasium. This new building was constructed perpendicularly to the back of the original school. Local citizens helped build it with lumber from the Mineral Mill. The gym was used unheated until 1953 when the student body increased to a point where two teachers were needed, and the building was converted to a regular classroom.

My husband, George, served on the school board from 1960 to 1973. He influenced the board to purchase the lot adjacent to the school, and he was instrumental in erecting a new facility in 1972. This new building, designed by Ben Kinikin, an architect from Sacramento, was a great innovation and asset for the community. In addition to two more classrooms, the building had a large common room that served as a gymnasium and community center with kitchen facilities. At this time there were over 40 students in the school. Al Schneider became Chief Ranger for Lassen Park in 1972 and brought with him his love of basketball. He organized a boys' team and, when he needed an opposing team for practice, organized the girls. My two younger girls were lucky to have him for a coach.

When I served on the school board in 1974 to 1978, we had difficulty finding housing for our teachers because there were no rentals available. The school board was able to purchase a house on Mineral Avenue that was used for several years. Later I was able to perfect a trade for a home adjacent to the school, the land of which could be used for expansion later if necessary. Unfortunately, the student body of the Mineral School decreased over time until only five students remained in 2005. The school board was at a loss as to what to do about the situation. Finally, in 2013, the Mineral District along with Paynes Creek and Manton Districts consolidated with the Antelope District in Red Bluff. As of 2015, the Mineral School is closed. Students are transported to Paynes Creek to attend school. What the future holds for the buildings is unknown at this time.

The decline in students is, I believe, a result of government change in policy regarding their employee housing. The Department of Interior, which administers Lassen Park, and the California Department of Transportation (CalTrans) had always provided housing for the majority of their employees because local housing was not usually available or adequate. This worked well for the employees because government rents were low, and they could save money to purchase a home when they retired. All this changed as the price of housing increased year after year, and the government rents increased until they were no longer a bargain, leaving a retiring employee with little purchasing power to buy a home on the open market. Today, most top employees for these agencies live either in Red Bluff or Chester and commute to work.

Adding to the loss of students for the Mineral School is also fewer employees at Mineral Lodge, the closing of the Mineral Mill, and lack of other business enterprises in the area. Another factor is changing attitudes about living in a rural area. People want to be where there is more action and more people. When I tell people I grew up in Mineral, their mouths drop and they say, "I can't believe you grew up in MINERAL," like I came from Mars. It is hard to explain what a great community it was with all the advantages that are not valued today.

Social life in Mineral was centered on the school. Holiday events such as Halloween, Christmas, and Easter always took place there. The main event of the year was the Christmas program where the students sang, recited, and acted in one or two plays. In my day, the back of the classroom was used as a stage with a makeshift curtain strung along a fourth of the room. The audience sat on folding chairs or at the students' desks. Each student had one or two parts in the chosen play, and everyone sang the Christmas carols at the end of the program. Every teacher I had could play the piano, which was necessary to drown out the off-key singers like myself. Santa Claus arrived and distributed gifts. Students drew names so everyone gave a gift and received one. Homemade refreshments, provided by parents, were served afterwards.

Christmas performance at the Mineral School, c. 1970s

Halloween was another big event when my children were attending the Mineral School. The students wore costumes that were judged by a panel of adults while they paraded around the school. The costumes had to be homemade in order to win a prize. The best one I ever made was an angel with wings for my oldest daughter, Heidi.

Skiing on Friday afternoons was started by Gabriel Brown, who had the school adopt a large sugar pine with a diameter of 25 feet. This tree is located off a logging road about four or five miles from Mineral. Gabriel persuaded the Forest Service not to let the tree be harvested, and students kept the trail open for many years. Without the school's protection, the tree will no doubt be lumber in a new home someday.

It is disappointing to know my favorite school is closed and may never hear the laughter of children again. But I still have wonderful memories of my time spent attending the school, and my many efforts supporting it. ℘

THE MINERAL MILL

When the Mineral Lodge burned down in 1939, it was a big financial loss for my parents. To make matters worse, a large insurance policy had not been paid, so there was little money to rebuild. My father, Husky, elected to use the only resource he had left—timber. This was the tall pine, cedar, and fir trees on the 480 acres originally purchased by his father and Warren Woodson. Since there was no lumber mill in or near Mineral, Husky persuaded Sam Crowley, who operated a mill in Quincy, to relocate that mill to Mineral. Crowley was an excellent operator and, not only logged all our timber, but much more in the surrounding area. The mill produced one inch thick, rough-sawn planks that were used for bomb racks during World War II. You can still see this siding on some of the homes in Cool Air that were built during that time. The mill was located on the north side of Hwy 36 across from where the sewer ponds are today. It was a small mill, with a pond for logs and a burn pile for the parts of logs not used. It produced approximately 750 board feet per day and operated until 1946–47 when Crowley moved his operations to Richfield near Corning.

Loading logs in the woods (courtesy Betty Brown)

I remember visiting the mill sometime after it first started operations. I have never forgotten the experience. The huge logs, three to five feet in diameter cut in lengths of 20 feet, were placed in a position so that a carriage with a large circular saw ran the length of the log, cutting off a slice. The slice was then cut into one foot boards and sent by a chain to the side of the mill where men pulled the boards off the chain and stacked them for drying. The mechanism that sent the boards forward was called the green chain. Wood pieces that were not usable were sent to the burn pile. Logs waiting to be cut were kept in the pond beside the mill. As I remember, a man rode and directed the carriage that sawed the logs. It was noisy and dangerous work.

I was attending the Mineral School during the years of the Crowley mill operation. They were felling the marketable trees in Cool Air and the Battle Creek Meadows property adjacent to the school. We watched many a tree fall with a loud crash. It made school very exciting. We also had great fun running on top of the logs after the limbs had been removed. The surface was not smooth and challenged our dexterity. We could not wait to run as fast as we could.

Brown sawmill (courtesy Betty Brown)

In the spring of 1948, the Mineral Mill was in operation again under the ownership of the Brown brothers, Harvey, Dick, and Phil, who had grown up in Westwood, California, and in mining towns all over the west, from Virginia City, Nevada, to Bodie, California. The Browns traced their ancestry to William the Conqueror. Harvey, the oldest, had been a merchant seaman before and during World War II; Dick had been in the 10th Mountain Division; and Phil had been a pilot in the Air Force. I have a chair that Harvey made for my father out of Philippine mahogany wood from one of his voyages.

Harvey married Betty Schmidt from Ross, California, whose father had owned and operated Schmidt Lithographic in San Francisco. Dick's wife, Minki, was an Austrian whom he met in Europe during the war. Phil's wife, Mary Alice, was a local Mineral lady whose father, Ross Parker, had constructed many homes in Mineral.

All three families lived in Mineral as long as the mill was operating, and they contributed much to the social and economic life of the town. Using Mineral Mill lumber, they constructed a building to house the fire truck

Harvey Brown with large tree cut (courtesy Betty Brown)

behind the Mineral Garage and also a gym for the Mineral School. They helped operate the small rope-tow next to Mineral Lodge and were instrumental in organizing the National Ski Patrol and Junior Ski Patrol at the Lassen Park Ski Area. Harvey was the first fire chief for the Mineral Volunteer Fire Department, and the families helped with its organization and operation. They plowed the roads in the winter for the community with their equipment and were always ready to help anybody and everybody in the area. They were truly "Good Neighbors" and much more.

The Brown's mill suffered a devastating fire on May 31, 1950. They rebuilt and continued operating until 1957 when they were forced to close due to lack of timber. Both Crowley and the Browns were cutting trees on Diamond National land. When Diamond put a mill in Lyman Springs and one in Red Bluff, the company no longer allowed other mills to harvest their timber.

Lumber mill crew (courtesy Betty Brown)

MINERAL HOSE COMPANY NO. 1

The name of the volunteer fire department in Mineral has always been fascinating to me. Why a hose company, not a fire company? And the use of No. 1? With the size of Mineral at the time, population 85, the possibility of No. 2 was remote. The reason for the unique name makes good sense when the circumstances are known. Early in 1950, when the community felt they needed some organization to fight fires, the first step was taken by my father who owned and operated the water company that supplied the subdivisions that were Mineral. He installed one and one-half inch standpipes throughout the area for use with hoses in case of a fire. Since all that was available were hoses, it seemed like a good name to use.

On June 2, 1950, the Mineral Hose Co. No. 1 was given a charter from the county. Twenty-one men over the age of 18, most of the able-bodied men in the community, signed the original charter. That original roster listed the following members: William Hayes, Hugh Fields, Lester Bodine, Harvey Brown, Philip Brown, Richard Brown, Charles Edwards, Paul Becker, William Douglas, Ross Parker, Ernest Schultz, Chris Hafley, Alfred Wilson, Walter Wilson, Cyril Wilson, Robert Smith, William Warren, Alfred Donau, Merrill Woodward, Walter Lane, and H. K. Beresford. This was the first volunteer fire company in Tehama County.

The impetus for the Hose Co. No. 1 was the second Mineral Lodge fire and other events that occurred in January of 1949. That night in January everyone available had been called to help, but a better system was needed. Money was a problem as there were no public funds, and landowners could not be taxed for this purpose. Potlucks and other fundraising events were put on by the women of the community, and a letter was sent asking all landowners to donate $35 each for the new enterprise. In May 1950, a 1936 Dodge pumper was purchased from Tehama County for $400. It could pump 50 gallons of water per minute, so who cared how old it was? It was painted bright red with the proud logo on it. A garage to house this wonder was constructed with volunteer labor and lumber donated by the Mineral Mill. A loud siren was installed on the roof of the service station as the fire engine's garage was located on the same property.

When the siren sounded, all members of Hose Co. No. 1, as well as the rest of the community, turned out to help. On a cold night in February of our first winter, the fire siren sounded. My husband, George, who had been raised in Chicago, could not believe that he had to get up and fight fire at that hour of the night. I finally convinced him that it was his duty whether he liked it or not. "Welcome to a small community." The fire was the Dick Brown house, and when it looked like they might not save the house, George and others were asked to move the furniture outside. He asked me later, "Why move that old stuff?" The old stuff was 18th century, antique chests that Gabrielle Brown had brought from Austria when she came to America as a war bride in 1944.

The original charter did not allow the Hose Company to fight any fires further than two miles from the community. Since that original charter, the communities of Mill Creek, Childs Meadows, Deer Creek, and Fire Mountain Lodge have been added. There are now two fire engines—the larger one at the CalTrans yard in Mineral and a small pumper in Mill Creek. The siren no longer sounds as members are called up by radio scanners. The Hose Company also acts as first responder for any other type of emergency. All volunteers are trained in first aid; three members are EMTs. Today in 2016, there are only seven volunteer members. To become a volunteer requires 100 hours of training. Al Blumquist is Fire Chief with Terry Neher as assistant.

Funding for Hose Co. No. 1 has been solved by the pancake breakfast at Mill Creek Resort on July 4th every year. The fundraiser was started in 1984 and has become so popular that over 500 people attended in 2016. The event now includes raffles and a parade, which last year even had two floats. Everyone has a great time raising money.

Skier George Perkins (W. L. Stillwell Photography)

CHAPTER 15

SKIING

It is seldom that we have ever seen a course like the one provided on the slopes of Mt. Baldy for the slaloms and downhill races. Not a tree to mar the giant slopes and an undulating terrain of clean, deep snow seems to stretch up into the sky. A large crowd climbed up through the cedars and sugar pines laden with their tufts of snow, along isles through the forest to the course and was it worth it? Indeed it was!

California Ski News, Tuesday, March 1, 1938

It is difficult to imagine that the official California State Ski Championship tournament was actually held in Mineral that year. It is even harder to believe that the races were held on Mt. Baldy and that the spectators had to walk over a mile to watch the event. Mt. Baldy today does not fit its name because trees now mar its perfect ski slope. In 1938 the mountain was bald because a forest fire had stripped it of all its timber and only brush covered its slope, thus making it very suitable for what was then referred to as "The Down Mountain Race." To locate Mt. Baldy today take Hwy 172 from Mineral to Mill Creek. As you approach the bridge over Battle Creek, look up to the left where 11 would be on a clock. The ski

Mt. Baldy, site of the 1938 State Ski Champion Tournament (Eastman Studio)

jump was located on the bottom section of Mt. Baldy. At one time, the Mineral dump was just in front of this steep hill. Due to the growth of trees, it is difficult to see either of these sites today.

The largest field of contestants ever assembled in the history of California skiing entered this event in 1938. The field totaled 109 men and women from ski clubs as far away as Los Angeles. There are conflicting newspaper accounts as to the number of spectators watching the race—one estimate was of 2,000 people; a second mentioned 700 spectators. I tend to believe the latter figure because of the difficulty getting to the site. The Reno Ski Club had two contestants who are of some interest today. Marty Arrouge married Norma Shearer, a famous Hollywood movie star, and Wayne Paulson later purchased the land that is today Squaw Valley. The Auburn Ski Club's Roy Mikkelsen, a member of the 1932 Olympic Ski team, won the Class-A jumping.

This was not the first ski tournament held in the area. On April 8, 1934, a so-called "Amateur Ski Tournament" was held in Lassen Park. There were a grand total of 38 contestants for the ski jumping, slalom, and down mountain race. The races started at the top of 8,000-foot Eagle Peak and ended on frozen Lake Helen. The 500 spectators drove through 25-foot snowbanks to get to the area. This was the deepest snow ever recorded since they started keeping records in 1931. It was the one and only time that the Lassen Park loop highway has been open in the wintertime.

On April 8, 1935, 50 hardy racers competed in Mineral on Mt. Baldy. Few people watched this race due to heavy rain that prevented the ski jumping from being held. This tournament was supposed to be held at the Sulphur Works but had been switched to Mineral because of the weather.

All of these events, and subsequent ones, were held by the Mt. Lassen Ski Club of Mineral. The club was organized in the winter of 1930–31. My father, Husky, is listed as being the most active of the individuals who first organized the club and was the first treasurer. Husky believed in skiing and just knew that it would become the sport that it is today. He did everything in his power to promote the sport in the North State. The first real event the club sponsored was a professional ski jumping exhibition in January of 1932. Husky constructed a 50-meter ski jump that was also used in the 1938 tournament for this exhibition. The eight jumpers were mostly Norwegian with the names of Engen and Ulland, except for Ted Rex who came from Michigan. These jumpers introduced the first real knowledge of how to turn and wax skis. In 1933, the jumpers returned in January, and the first annual invitational tournament for amateur skiers was held in February of that year. This tournament is noteworthy because it incorporated the first "Down Mountain" or downhill straight race held in California. The course was on Mt. Baldy.

The area around Lassen Peak attracted skiers because of the record snowfalls and the fact that the snow stayed on the high peaks well into the summer months. This fostered a mid-summer ski tournament appropriately called the "Lassen Inferno." The first race, according to the history of the club, was held on August 14,

Lassen Inferno Race with downhill course outlined

1938. This race began on the summit of Lassen Peak, elevation 10,500 feet, and ended on the park road at 8,500 feet. According to Dave Altman who raced in 1948, the course had only four gates and two turns. The unusual feature of the race was the jumping of the park road. A racer could take a slower route over a man-made bridge to the finish line, or he could jump the road, the faster route. Dick Brown is the jumper in the famous photo of this era. On July 4, 1942, this race was held under the able direction of Dr. Frank Howard and Albert Sigal of the California Ski Association. During World War II, no races were held because most of the top skiers joined the 10th Mountain Division.

The last mid-summer ski race was held in 1948. I should remember because I participated in the slalom. I remember being so scared because I had been skiing since I was five, and I felt I should have been a better skier than I was. As it turned out, I missed a gate and was disqualified, ending my racing career.

The Mt. Lassen Ski Club was so successful because of local volunteers, not only from Mineral, but also from the surrounding

Lassen Inferno Race—Dick Brown jumping over road (Eastman Studio)

communities of Red Bluff, Corning, Chico, and Westwood. Max Stewart from Red Bluff; Gene Barton, Chief Ranger from Lassen Park; and Albert Wahl, Lassen Park's commissioner were some of the first organizers. The women were called to serve coffee and donuts and to be scorekeepers. The club had over 200 members and was able to sponsor skiers to other tournaments throughout California. Lassen was well represented in the World Champion Ski Jump in the Los Angeles Coliseum in 1938–39. Si Brand from Westwood was an Olympic class skier. I found his name in the National Ski Museum in New Hampshire. The Mt. Lassen Ski Club also sponsored a "snow bus" from the San Francisco Bay area to Lassen in 1939. How long this service lasted, I am not sure. At the same time, they were giving free ski school and free ski rentals to high school students from Corning, Hamilton City, Chico, and Orland. Mineral Lodge provided the brightly painted red skis with large black numbers for free.

My father was such a fan of skiing that he supported some of the skiers such as Si Brand and the Brown Brothers during the winter months as most of them worked in the woods or mills in Westwood during the summer months. My mother did not take kindly to this charity of Husky's, but she put up with it. One story I was told by Betty Brown, Harvey's wife, is that they were to provide their own wood for heat in the free rental cabin that Husky provided to them. Their solution was to pick up the wood from Husky's woodpile and carry it to their cabin.

The early interest and enthusiasm in skiing is gone today from Mineral and Lassen Park. The early skiers came because of the terrain and the snow, but the National Park was off-limits for development, so the big movers and shakers of yesterday moved on to the Sierras. In the 1940s, Hannes Schroll and others who had been early skiers at Lassen built the Sugar Bowl Ski Area in Norden, California, the first ski area with a chair lift.

I met my husband, George Perkins, in Denver, Colorado, where I was stationed as a stewardess for United Air Lines. We skied in the mountains west of Denver and were active in the Ski Patrol. When we became engaged to be married, my father and mother came to visit and discuss our future in Mineral. The Lassen Park Company had been operating a rope-tow in Lassen Park since 1935 (except for the war years) and had decided to move the operation to the north side of the park because it would be closer to Manzanita Lake Lodge, which they owned and operated. This move would be devastating financially to Mineral Lodge as most winter business depended upon skiing, and skiing needed some sort of uphill transportation. My father felt that he would be able to sublease the winter operation from the Lassen Park Company as he was a good friend of Biz Johnson from Roseville who represented our area in the House of Representatives. Husky did not want to take on such a project without more help from the family. At that time only fools and ardent skiers went in to the ski business because there was little profit. This all changed after the 1960 Winter Olympics in Squaw Valley, but this was 1954. Even so, we were hooked on skiing, felt adventurous, and had no fear, so of course we said yes.

My father had operated a rope-tow on the hill west of the Lodge for several years beginning in 1939 with great success. In fact, I believe that was the first ski area to offer night skiing when lights were installed. Christie Hill, which is between Mineral and the Park entrance, once had a rope-tow operated by the Mt. Lassen Ski Club in 1938 and again in 1946 by the Altman's. The elevation of both areas was not high enough to ensure snow for most of the ski season. Mineral is 5,000 feet; Christie Hill is 5,600.
George and I were married in Mineral in 1955 and lived in Colorado Springs until my father could work out the ten-year lease with the federal government and the Lassen Park Company. The ski business being what it was, the lease was written with more terms if we failed than if we were successful. Actually, we were very successful, and we had a lot of fun doing it.

We installed a Poma-like lift that took skiers up a very steep hill called "The Face." The lift consisted of plastic disks suspended from a cable that skiers straddled and leaned on to be pulled up. We also

Mineral Ski Hill west of the Lodge, c. 1936 (Eastman Studio)

had two rope-tows, one intermediate and one we called the Bunny Hill, which was only about 100 feet long.

The so-called Ski Hut was a real piece of work. It had been a CCC barracks that measured approximately 15 x 30 feet, with a lean-to of maybe 10 x 15 feet on the side. It had a rough, unfinished, wood floor that was always wet from the snow. An area of 15 x 10 feet at the back of the building was used for food service. We used the lean-to for renting skis. The main part of the building had a wood stove made from an old oil drum surrounded by a pipe structure covered with chicken wire used for drying wet gloves and to keep people from being burned if the fire was too hot. Wood was stored under the building and had to be thrown up every morning for that day's use. Three or four tables and chairs were near the food service with built-in benches on the inside walls. The wood stove was the only heat except for an oil heater in the ski rental area. We were open three days a week: Friday, Saturday, and Sunday.

We arrived to this unheated building with the temperatures usually below freezing. We had to light the gas hot-water heater (you know, hold the knob in until it stays lit), throw the day's wood supply up, install five gallons of oil for the heater and light it, and sweep the still wet or frozen floor. I was forbidden to sell sunflower seeds because those little seeds would not sweep up easily and stayed mired in the muck on the floor. The restroom facilities were vaulted pit-style shelters located in the parking area, not near the Ski Hut. We served hamburgers, hot dogs, chili beans, tuna and deviled egg sandwiches, coffee, hot chocolate, and canned sodas. We kept the sodas cold in an old, wooden icebox. There was just enough generator electricity for overhead lights and a coffee pot.

We spent a great deal of effort promoting the ski area to increase business. Two Red Bluff high school teachers, Carl Coleman and Allen Peters, who were also skiers, helped persuade the Red Bluff High School to send a bus every Saturday for their students to enjoy skiing. We also had buses from other schools in the valley at different times. We hired Eric Johnson in Berkeley to assist us with advertising; he designed brochures, stationary, and other material. Eric, a native of Finland, was an excellent artist and a professional ski instructor. Through him, we were able to meet other ski area managers and operators. One of the hardest tasks we had was to educate the public concerning the weather. When it was foggy in the valley, it was a beautiful day in the mountains, and the skiing was great. We initiated a Family Pass: for $45 a family could ski for the whole year. This idea, which was George's, was one of the things that helped make the enterprise a success. The price was so cheap, families could not afford to ski any place else. They usually brought extra kids along and purchased daily tickets as well. By the end of our ten-year lease, we had large crowds of people from valley towns as far away as Sacramento, and the price of the family pass had increased to $150. During the Christmas Holidays and on weekends, we filled Mineral Lodge, which was one of our goals.

We belonged to the Sierra Ski Areas Association and attended monthly meetings held in different areas. Members of this association were all unique entrepreneurs who had worked hard to put their particular ski area on the map. They were a dynamic

Promotional poster for the Lassen Park Ski Area by Eric Johnson

group; everyone struggled to make a profit in a very difficult business that depended on the weather a lot of the time. If it did not snow enough, the business was in trouble; if it snowed too much, the business was in even worse trouble. One year, we had over 32 feet of snow at the Ski Area and had to close for the season. There was just too much snow.

We teamed up with Pat Murdock, who owned a small bed and breakfast in Mount Shasta, to promote our two areas at the San Francisco Ski Show. He was an excellent carpenter and a great promoter, so we had attractive booths to work from. One year he gave a cocktail party in a local hotel with a topless cocktail waitress. This was a big hit.

George gave ski reports to the radio stations every Thursday and Friday nights, giving the depth of snow, the temperature, current conditions, and the up-coming weather report—anything and everything to put our name before the public. We were able to have quite a few nice articles in major newspapers, one article in the *Berkeley Gazette* had pictures of the whole family. Our biggest coup featured George and our five-year-old daughter, Heidi, on the cover of *Ski Magazine* with the title "Ski a Volcano."

We received a great deal of help from individuals in Mineral and the surrounding communities. Lester Bodine had been an avid skier since his first employment as a temporary ranger for the National Park Service in Mineral. He refused to be transferred to any other National Park because of his great love of Lassen and skiing. In the early years of skiing, regional ski clubs like the Mt. Lassen Ski Club were the main supporters and sponsors of skiing, but ski club importance gradually faded to be replaced by business owners as the ski industry developed. Skiing was, and still is, somewhat of a dangerous sport subject to injuries by those participating. Members of the ski clubs recognized this and usually took care of all injuries. The National Ski Patrol system developed from this need for help in caring for the injured, especially removing them from the ski hill. Members of a Ski Patrol were required to have a valid Red Cross first aid certificate and a certain proficiency in skiing. The owners of ski areas needed this help to run a good area, so skiing was provided free to Ski Patrol members. It was prestigious to be a member of a Ski Patrol. Lester Bodine was head of the patrol in Lassen when we took over the area, and he was prominent in the National Ski Patrol system. He very definitely made our job easier by running a tight ship and by offering assistance any place and everywhere. He was a great supporter of the ski area and helped to promote it in the valley towns wherever he went.

Wally Stillwell from Red Bluff loved to ski, and he was a good photographer. He was on the ski slopes every weekend and took a great many photos, which he printed for us. We had an ample supply for publicity and decorated the back bar at Mineral Lodge with them. Wally was not married and rather shy. We just knew we had the perfect date for him in Helen, who was a secretary for the Park Service and lived in Mineral. We finally talked him into coming to a party in the government recreation hall where we had numerous parties and lots of fun. He was introduced to Helen

Lassen Park Ski Area, c. 1959

several times, and they did live happily ever after with their three children in Red Bluff.

Sadly for us, our ten-year lease had not been written with options for additional years on the contract, and the federal government did not want us to continue because the Lassen Park Company made a profit on our lease. We paid them 3.5%; they paid the Government only 1.5%. In the summer of 1966 we were told to remove our Poma lift within 30 days. George traveled to the Sierras to peddle a used Poma lift. He was not having much success and thought about not stopping at Squaw Valley, which was then the largest ski area, because it was so large and probably could not even use a Poma lift. But he decided not to leave a stone unturned and called on the manager who said he wasn't interested, but gave George the idea to sell the lift to a ski club. Luckily, the ski club in nearby Chester was very interested, and they had the manpower to remove the lift for us. So we were out of the ski business, which we had truly enjoyed.

Losing the ski area was a blow emotionally and financially, but we felt that we still had Mineral Lodge and additional land for further

Sky jumper Si Brand

development. And most importantly, we had established the ski area as a viable business for the future. How wrong we were! With a new Ski Chalet in 1966 and a three-person chairlift in 1982, the future looked good; however, competition from Mount Shasta Ski Park and lack of heavy snow at Lassen from 1986 to 1992 caused financial losses for California Guest Services who had replaced the old Lassen Park Company. They chose to close the area in 1993. I joined a coalition group to take over the operation but with no success. The National Park Service would not give us the time of day to even discuss the situation, and that was that.

Two years later, George and I invested in a ski rental business in South Lake Tahoe. This was very successful, and we were still in the ski business. ✧

The 50-meter ski jump Husky constructed in 1932. Here, people are watching a ski jumping championship at Mineral on February 17, 1935. (courtesy Dan Foster)

CHAPTER 16

LASSEN VOLCANIC NATIONAL PARK

Lassen Peak is the centerpiece of Lassen Volcanic National Park. This mountain was officially designated Lassen Peak in 1915 but had been called by earlier names. The Spanish named it Mt. Saint Joseph in 1821, and the Hudson's Bay explorers called it Snow Mountain. Early settlers referred to it and Brokeoff Mountain as Sister Buttes. The name Lassen comes from an early Danish pioneer, Peter Lassen, who was given a Mexican Land Grant near Vina (between Chico and Red Bluff) in 1844. He returned to Missouri in 1847 to lead an immigrant group over his new trail west using Lassen Peak as his guidepost. His trail never became popular because it went all the way north to Alturas from Nevada, then south and west to his Rancho where Deer Creek joins the Sacramento River. It is possible today to see evidence of this trail near Black Rock between Mill Creek and Deer Creek.

Peter Lassen was not a good businessman and later lost his land. He left the Sacramento Valley, settling near Susanville where he was active in politics. He was later murdered by an unknown assailant in northwest Nevada and is buried in the Susanville area.

In May 1907, President Theodore Roosevelt proclaimed both Cinder Cone and Lassen Peak as national monuments, both administrated by the National Forest Service, there being no National Park Service at that time. The area around Cinder Cone National Monument was approximately eight square miles and Lassen Peak National Monument included only the mountain. In 1912, the Lassen National Park Committee was formed to promote the area as a National Park. Michael Dittmar who established the first newspaper in Redding called the *Morning Searchlight*, A. L. Conard who owned the Tremont Hotel in Red Bluff, and Warren Woodson from Corning were members of this committee. Congressman John E. Raker from Susanville introduced a bill that year to establish Peter Lassen National Park. This bill failed as did subsequent bills in 1913 and 1914.

Things changed when Lassen Peak erupted in 1914 because it was the only active volcano in the continental United States and received a lot of notoriety. Both Houses of Congress passed a bill in 1916 designating the area as a National Park. The original bill included 79,561 acres; the Park covers 106,000 acres today.

This new National Park faced many challenges. There was no funding from Congress and no roads of any consequence. The new Park was not popular with cattlemen because grazing was not allowed in it. At one time, the Tehama County Board of Supervisors attempted to pass a resolution to abolish the Park in order to protect grazing rights. The Park committee kept Lassen's plight in the news. Congress finally appropriated $2,500 in 1920. The funds increased slowly until they were a modest $23,000 by 1929. The first ranger, Walker Collins, was hired in 1922 for $150 a month, and he had to provide his own horse. He was appointed the first superintendent of the Park in 1928.

The decision to place the Park headquarters in Mineral instead of at Manzanita Lake was made when the National Forest Service offered 80 acres of their land for the purpose. Michael Dittmar was opposed to this plan because it benefitted Redding to have the headquarters at Manzanita Lake. He also believed that Walter Collins had family and friends who would benefit from the Mineral

Lassen Peak erupting, c. 1915

headquarters. A. L. Conard disagreed. He felt that the government had made the right decision for reasons of economy between the Park Service and the Forest Service. It is interesting to note that Dittmar was correct about Collins who was married to my father's cousin and had grown up in Corning. Woodson and my grandfather had purchased the Mineral property in 1920. It definitely benefitted Mineral Lodge to have the Park headquarters in Mineral. Conard also owned land, still in possession of his descendants, near Mineral. Lassen Park has Mount Conard and Raker Peak but no mountain named for Dittmar.

Walker Collins, Lassen Park's first ranger, on Lassen Peak (courtesy Josh Dale)

Originally there were no roads through the Park or, for that matter, no approach roads either. In 1920-22, the Forest Service completed a road (with funds transferred from the Park Service) from Mineral to the Sulphur Works on a trail made by the Supan family. The Service declined to go any further with the road. The Department of Interior approved the present loop highway through the Park, but Congress did not approve any funds for the project at that time. The Lassen Park Association was able to obtain an appropriation of $8,000 from the State of California for engineering and road studies in 1923. The road was finally completed in 1931 with funds from Congress. A crowd of 15,000 attended the dedication of the nation's 13th National Park in July of that year. The event received national publicity because of a big advertising campaign to enact a fake eruption on Lassen Peak with rockets, flares, and smoke bombs. The largest crowd at Kings Creek Meadow was disappointed when all they heard was the sound—windy conditions blew the smoke to the north.

The first eruption of Lassen Peak occurred on May 30, 1914, and was first seen by a local cattleman, Bert McKenzie, who reported it to the Forest Service in Mineral. They determined he was correct as black smoke and steam were rising some 200 to 300 feet above the mountain. The next day, Forest Ranger Richard Abbey walked from Mineral via the Sulphur Works to the top of Lassen Peak. He discovered a crater blowing out steam and ash with loud hissing noises. He returned to Mineral that evening and reported his findings to his supervisor who then notified the local and national newspapers. Lassen Peak's eruption created worldwide interest—newspaper reporters and others flocked to the area. Most had no fear and immediately hiked up the mountain to see the eruption first hand.

We are lucky to have the wonderful photographic record of Lassen Peak's eruptions from B. F. Loomis. He was an early pioneer to the area around the mountain. He made wood shakes in the Manzanita Lake area, operated a sawmill, and owned and operated a hotel in Viola. Loomis purchased his first camera with a B&L Anastigmatic lens in 1897. He used this camera when Lassen Peak began to erupt. Loomis took elaborate, detailed photos of the many eruptions with great risk of life as he was often on the summit when the mountain was active. On June 9, 1914, he took a series of photographs progressing from the very beginnings of an eruption through to its completion. These photographs were published both in the United States and abroad.

Loomis Museum

Loomis had one daughter, Mae, who died at the early age of 21. The family built a museum of native stone and reinforced concrete in Mae's name and deeded the building, along with 40 acres to the Park in 1929. This museum is still in use today as a visitors' center and contains many photographs by Loomis. His wife, Estelle, painted watercolors over his black and white photographs to enhance them. The back section of the museum displayed these large, colored photos as a backdrop for stuffed animals that were native to the Park. As a child, I thought this was great and looked forward to seeing the display every time I visited the museum. Sadly the display is no longer there.

Lassen Peak continued to erupt until 1921. The most violent eruptions occurred in May 1915 when melted snow, ash, and debris created a destructive lahar that swept down five to six miles into the valleys of Hat Creek and Lost Creek. During this period, a hot blast, charged with dust and rock fragments, blew down trees on the slopes of Raker Peak three miles away.

During the eruptions, people came from near and far to see the activity. One interesting story concerns a group from Manton.

Lance Graham and some companions were on the summit during an eruption in June 1914. He and his friends were standing on the edge of the crater when his hat flew off. When he went to retrieve it, he was hit by falling rock. His companions assumed he was dead and ran back down the mountain. Another group went up to retrieve the body and found Graham alive but severely injured. He had suffered a concussion, deep cuts to his back, a broken collarbone, and three broken ribs. He recovered and vowed he would never climb Lassen Peak again and warned his family never to climb it either. It is interesting to note that Lance Graham's grandchildren still have the 5 x 2 1/2 inch piece of volcanic rock that was embedded in his shoulder.

Lassen Peak is described as a plug volcano—imagine a tube of toothpaste squeezed from below. It rose rapidly in very recent geologic time after the destruction of ancestral Mount Tehama. This former great mountain, considered the southernmost Cascade, had a base between 11 and 15 miles across and rose more than 11,000 feet above sea level. Over the years, the top of the mountain was destroyed forming a great bowl or caldera, with the Sulphur Works as its center. Brokeoff Mountain, at an elevation of 9,232, is the

Lassen Peak and relative location of ancient Mount Tehama

Brokeoff Mountain
(photograph by D.F. Barton, courtesy Dan Foster)

largest remnant of this old mountain. Looking east as you drive north from Red Bluff to Redding you can see Mount Diller on the north and Brokeoff Mountain on the south which gives an idea of the size of the ancient mountain.

When Lassen Park, was created it still contained acreage that was privately owned. The main areas were the resort in Drakesbad, building lots and cabins around Juniper Lake, and the Sulphur Works area. In the ensuing years, park superintendents, with the help of the Department of Interior, were able to purchase these properties for reasonable sums of money. The Siffords had developed Drakesbad in the early 1900s and sold it to the government in 1958. Juniper Lake had various owners until it was purchased in 1914 by a San Francisco attorney, Charles Snell, for $2,500. He developed and sold lots and built a lodge and cabins, which he ran in the summer months. His granddaughter finally sold the Snell's interest of 400 acres in 1957 for $99,750. However, there are still some cabins on lots developed by the Snells in private ownership. The Sulphur Works area had been obtained by Dr. Supan as early as 1885 under a mining claim. Interestingly, the Park built the loop highway, which we use today, right through the Supan land because Dittmar claimed he had obtained a right-of-way from the family for one dollar. Later it was discovered that he had failed to record the deed for this right-of-way. Over the years, different members of the Supan family built a service station, a restaurant, and a lodge with limited success. The most successful business was established by Don and Ed Supan who put themselves through college after World War II by selling souvenirs, especially a line they developed by putting the nearby unusual rocks from the outcroppings into a concentration of sulfuric acid overnight. The result was a beautiful, coral-like rock with delicate colors. The Supans sold their holding to the government for $48,960 in 1952.

In 1935, Superintendent Walker Collins was fired by the government over some financial accountability. My father told me that the Park had been allotted money to hire men for work in the Park, but no money was allotted for tools for the men to work with. To solve the problem, Collins obtained tools from Red Bluff merchants, listing the merchants' names as employees. The Government auditors were satisfied until they drove through Red Bluff and noticed that Walter Stoll was a business not a person. My father was a very truthful person, so I believe that is the true story. Unfortunately, Collins never recovered from his dismissal. His brother, George, who developed the idea of the fake Lassen Peak eruption at the dedication of the loop highway, went on to a successful career in the National Park Service.

In 1930, Western Pacific Railroad proposed to the Park Service to build a lodge at Manzanita Lake for $275, thus being Lassen Park's concessionaire. Due to the delay in establishing passenger service in their new Highline route and management changes, they backed out of the arrangement in 1932. Two local park rangers, Don Hummel and Charles Keathley, asked if they might be considered as the Park's only concessionaires. They were not given permission for such until they obtained financial backing from Dallas Dort of Phoenix, Arizona, who loaned them $10,000. They were granted a three-year lease and formed the Lassen National Park Company. In 1933, they built the Manzanita Lake Lodge along with nine cabins. Over the years, the Lassen Park Company prospered, building more cabins, a gift shop, and a general store. Keathley was replaced as general manager by Al Donau. The company was well-managed

Lassen Park South Entrance, c. 1930s (Eastman Studio)

and successful. Ownership was retained by Dallas Dort and Don Hummel.

In 1972, the Lassen Park Company sold all of their holding in Lassen Park to U. S. Resources, a mining corporation. The story was that they purchased the Lassen Park Company to enhance their image with the U. S. Government. The new owners were not happy with their purchase because they were not able to make the profits they had envisioned. A U. S. Geological Survey made in 1968 determined that a rockfall avalanche from unstable Chaos Crags, which lies north of Lassen Peak, could inundate the Manzanita Lake area. U. S. Resources informed the government that unless the government could insure people's lives in that area they could no longer keep the facilities at Manzanita Lake open. The government purchased all of the company's facilities in the Manzanita Lake area. U. S. Resources still owned and operated the Ski Area at the south end of the Park. A few years later, they claimed they could not make enough money with this one business and again were able sell to the U. S. Park Service.

In 1974, it was announced that all buildings in the Manzanita Lake area were to be torn down, even the Loomis Museum. Fortunately the museum escaped destruction and was reopened in 1991 when the Park celebrated its 75th anniversary. This wonderful old building is now on the National Register of Historic Places as it should be. Today the concessionaire operates a small store, gift shop, and cabins in the summer months, and the Manzanita Lake campground is open.

When U. S. Resources stepped away from operating the Lassen Ski Area, John Koeberer of California Guest Services was granted a temporary license to operate that business. In 1982, the Park Service announced that they were open to bids for a 20-year contract to operate all concessions in Lassen Park. I partnered with three other qualified people to bid for the contract. We were unsuccessful, and California Guest Services was granted the contract. I wonder how different my life would have been had we

Lassen Park winter snow, c. 1960 (Eastman Studio)

won the contract. But things often work out for the best, and I'd even forgotten about entering the bid until I began to write this part of Lassen Park's history. Later I was told by one Park official that the figures we had submitted concerning sales and profits were accurate and equal to those submitted by California Guest Services. That had been my contribution to the partnership.

Sometime after 1966, the Lassen Ski Chalet was built to replace the old CCC barrack building that had been used as a chalet since the late 1930s. This new building was a great improvement for that era with large windows facing the ski slopes, an adequate lunch facility, and the lower floor housing ski rentals and first aid station for the ski patrol. The building was used as a visitor center in the summer months since Lassen was one of the few parks without such a center. The building was condemned in 2003 and demolished in 2005 to make way for a new planned visitor center. Work began in 2007 on the 8,000-square-foot building to be built in the same location. It was completed and opened in 2008 with the marvelous name of Kohm-Yah-Mah-Nee, the Yahi Indian name for Lassen Peak. Lassen had gone over 90 years without such a facility, even if it is one of the oldest National Parks.

The federal government passed the Wilderness Act in 1964. This led to a lot of controversy over how much of Lassen Park would be designated as wilderness since the entire Park acreage would qualify. Organizations such as The Sierra Club pushed for the maximum while local interests were against such action. President Richard Nixon signed the Lassen Volcanic Wilderness in 1972 after a compromise was reached among the various parties. Today 78,982 acres of the Park falls under this Act, can never be developed, and must remain in its natural state.

In 1931, when the loop highway was dedicated, 56,833 visitors were counted for the year. Visitation increased over the years and reached its highest number of 504,641 in 1972. Since then, the numbers declined to 468,092 in 2015. However, visitation in all National Parks has declined in the past 10 to 15 years. What is in store for my favorite National Park is certainly unknown since you can never predict the future. Maybe Lassen will erupt again. But I am certain it will always be there in one form or another for all of us to enjoy. ☙

Lassen Peak seen from Manzanita Lake

SPICE

Lester Bodine

Lester Bodine was an institution in Mineral. He first arrived in 1933 to work for the National Park Service as a laborer. Lester had been a stockbroker in Pasadena, but he never returned to that profession once he discovered Lassen Park. He worked many jobs in the winter and summer until he was hired as a temporary ranger in 1946. He achieved permanent ranger status in 1949 and was appointed Chief Ranger in 1967, a post he held until his retirement in 1969. He was offered many promotions to other National Parks but refused all of them. He knew where his heart belonged—it was Mineral and Lassen Volcanic National Park.

Lester's career with the National Park Service was only one facet of his life. He was an avid skier and worked on the Ski Patrol during the 1960 Olympics in Squaw Valley. He was appointed National Ski Patrolman of the year in 1960-61. He loved to teach first aid and was given a plaque by the American Red Cross in 1967 for teaching advanced first aid to over

1,000 people. He was also president of the Tehama County Community Concert Association for several years.

Lester and his wife, Muriel, made their home in Mineral, but they were known throughout the Sacramento Valley. They never missed a meeting or an event regardless of the weather; he drove somewhere at least two or three times a week. He always had time to do errands for anybody who asked and some who did not ask. If you needed a favor or a special prescription, Lester would be happy to help you. When Glenn Fuller passed away, his wife, Helen, had never written a check before. Lester taught her how to write checks and manage her finances. He had a deep interest in the children of Mineral and taught many of them to ski. It is hard to portray the humor, warm friendliness, and thoughtfulness of Lester, but I cannot think of him without a smile on my face.

Lester's "spice" was driving fast, and that he did. You did not want to meet him on a curve if you were over the white line. He did not waste time getting to where he wanted to go. One time, he and Muriel were late for a Lassen Transit trip. The bus left without them, so Lester just drove fast up I–5 until he caught up with the bus and somehow managed to signal the driver to stop at the next exit. They joined the trip there.

Muriel was older than Lester by a few years and suffered from various ailments, but she did not stay home. He took her to every event just as before. One of my friends considered this elder abuse, but I don't think so. Muriel enjoyed every minute of it. They both had varied interests in all sorts of thing: gardening, cooking, local history. When I visited them once, there was not a vacant chair to sit on because they were all filled with papers. So I stood—they did not even notice.

When Lester developed a life threatening illness, he moved them both to a convalescent hospital in Red Bluff where he used the telephone to keep up with his world because he could no longer drive. Muriel just faded away mentally after his death.

Life gives you very few Lester Bodines, and I feel very lucky to have had him around most of my life.

Lester active in the Lassen Park ski patrol, March 17, 1990

Turner Mountain Lookout

CHAPTER 17

MOUNTAIN LOOKOUTS

I cannot remember when lookouts were not a part of my life in Mineral. Turner Mountain is southwest of Mineral and Brokeoff Mountain is located in Lassen Park. Both of these mountains had operating lookout stations during the summer months, and both could only be reached by horseback or walking. Turner Mountain was named for the Turner family who were early settlers in the Lyonsville area; Brokeoff is named for its appearance, it being what is left of ancient Mount Tehama. I took many trips to both of these lookouts and enjoyed every minute of the adventures.

Lookout stations came into use after the United States suffered a series of devastating forest fires in 1910. The U. S. Forest Service, under the Department of Agriculture, supplied and maintained these stations. They first used tall trees located on high mountain tops with a good view of the surrounding terrain to detect fires; later they erected small buildings. A single employee was hired for the season, beginning May through October, depending on how early the rains arrived. The lookout employee usually worked for four weeks without a break, then had four days off before returning to the post. There was a telephone line from the lookout to headquarters so a fire could be reported as quickly as possible.

Once a fire was sighted by the lookout, he or she pinpointed the exact geographic location by the use of an Osborne Fire Finder. This device was invented by William Bushnell Osborne, Jr., in 1911 and is still used today. The Fire Finder consists of a topographic area map mounted on a rotating steel disc with attached sighting mechanisms that the operator can look through and find the exact location to report to headquarters. The device was located in the center of the building.

The Turner Mountain lookout building was installed in 1912 by the famous ranger, Richard Harvey Abbey. The lookout house was pre-constructed in Red Bluff and made collapsible so it could be transported to its location via pack animal using light lumber, preferably shiplap, for siding, 2 x 4s for studding and framework. The longest pieces were the four rafters that were nine feet long. The house was 10 x 10 feet with solid walls four feet in height and eight feet to the eaves. Glass windows filled the balance of space on all sides of the house. At one time there were lookouts on Lassen Peak and Brokeoff Mountain in Lassen Volcanic National Park. Ranger Abbey installed the lookout building on Lassen Peak the

Osborne Fire Finder, c. 1938 (United States Department of Agriculture)

Lassen Peak Lookout. (Top) December 10, 1914, with Ranger Abbey and Bert Hampton. (Bottom) Spring 1915 (courtesy Dan Foster)

same year he erected the one on Turner Mountain. The building on Lassen Peak was destroyed by a series of volcanic eruptions after the initial eruption in 1914; the Brokeoff lookout remained in use until sometime in the 1940s.

Turner Mountain Lookout station (right side)

On the back side of Turner Mountain, my father had a cabin that he used for deer hunting in the fall of the year. At that time, the only access to the mountain was a five mile trail maintained by the Forest Service. My father usually kept 10 to 12 horses in order to transport hunters and their supplies to his cabin. He hit on a great idea when it came to transporting those supplies to the cabin. He allowed the local elementary students to lead a loaded horse to the cabin for the privilege of riding the horse home. The kids thought it was great as they all were excited to ride horses. I did it once when I was about 12. I did not think it was fun. After that, any trips for me to the top of Turner were horseback both ways. Over the years in my many trips to both Turner and Brokeoff, it was always interesting to talk to the person who was manning the lookout.

When the Forest Service rescinded my father's permit for the cabin in the early 1960s and it was to be torn down, I did walk up there with my husband, George, who had never seen the cabin before. We took our black Airedale-looking dog, Clyde, and backpacks to spend the night. In previous years, black bears had broken into the cabin and caused some damage. When we arrived late in the

Brokeoff Mountain Lookout (Eastman Studio)

afternoon, Clyde sniffed around, immediately went into the cabin, secured himself under a bunk bed, and never uttered a sound or moved the entire night. He smelled the bears and was scared to death. We were not bothered by any—maybe the bears were afraid of Clyde.

A road was built to the Turner Mountain lookout sometime in the 1980s. A new tower was built at that time. The road helped in maintaining and supplying the lookout, although it has not been used as such for the past few years because of the age of the living facility and the fear of Hantavirus. Now, however, the Forest Service is faced with the quandary that the building is considered "historic." It cannot be torn down, and it can't be used. The trail from Mineral to the lookout is no longer passable. My daughter Heidi and I tried to hike to it a few years ago. We did not reach the summit because of her son's distress over bugs. It wasn't an easy hike, as the trail had not been maintained, and we had to climb over 50 logs. We covered three-quarters of the trail. Today I doubt if the trail can be located.

The use of fire lookouts has fallen in disfavor with the use of satellites. Currently, the Forest Service maintains the Bald Mountain lookout in Butte County and the Inskip lookout in Tehama County. The National Park Service staffs Mt. Harkness in the eastern part of Lassen Park. McCarthy Point lookout, located on the southern edge of the Mill Creek Rim facing north overlooking the scenic Mill Creek Canyon and the Ishi Wilderness, has been restored and is for rent through the Almanor Ranger District. It can be accessed by auto. The cost was $75 per night, with a two night minimum, in 2014.

Robert Harvey Abbey

Robert Harvey Abbey was a Forest Ranger from 1905 to 1932. He spent part of his service working for the Lassen National Forest, which had their summer headquarters in Mineral. He was a very capable, unusual man who could and did walk great distances as part of his job.

Abbey was hired in 1905 as a forest guard for the Forest Service under the Department of Agriculture. His pay was $900 per annum, and he was to provide his own horse and riding equipment. The extensive test he took to qualify for the job is quite interesting. The testing took three days and consisted of the following: marksmanship with a rifle and a revolver, chopping down small trees with an axe, packing equipment on a pack animal, saddling and riding a horse, finding a blaze on a tree in a dense forest, running a line using a compass, and estimating the board feet in a stand of growing timber on a 20-acre tract of land. I cannot imagine any government giving that test today.

He was working in the Mohawk Valley in Plumas County on April 18, 1906, when he was awakened by the shaking of the barn he was sleeping in. This was the great San Francisco earthquake that he had felt over 200 miles away.

To report for work in that same year, he took the horse drawn stage from his home in Oroville to Quincy. The trip cost $10 for the 65 miles and took between two and three days depending on the weather. There were nine passengers at the beginning of the journey, so his seat was in the "hurricane deck" on the top of the coach with the luggage until some of the passengers reached their destination. Part of the journey was on a sleigh due to snow on the road. The sleigh was pulled by horses equipped with snowshoes

In 1911, he was transferred to Lassen National Forest where he spent the summers in Mineral repairing telephone lines, installing lookout stations, and working on the local trails. Living in Red Bluff during the winter, he made frequent trips to Mineral to shovel the snow off the roofs of the Forest Service buildings. To make the trip to Mineral he rode the U. S. Mail Stage to Paynes Creek and traveled the remaining 19 miles on skis or snow shoes.

Abbey was working in Mineral on May 14, 1914, when he was alerted by his supervisor that Lassen Peak was erupting. He decided that he must see for himself what was happening, so he left the next morning at 4:00 a.m. on foot from the ranger station. He estimated that the trail to the top of Lassen was 15 or 16 miles. There was no snow the first five miles of the Forest Service trail until he reached Morgan Summit at 5,600 feet elevation. Past the summit the snow was four feet deep. He continued on, crossing several large streams of water with the snow eight to ten feet high on either side. After passing the Sulphur Works, the snow was frozen into ice, so he had to chop steps with his belt axe to continue. He reached the top of the ridge on Lassen Peak by 10:00 a.m. and could look down into the crater. Steam and ashes were being blown out in puffs; loud noises and hissing steam could be heard from the crater. He then hiked down into the crater where he could see approximately 50 feet down. He could see small round holes on the side of the crater where steam was gushing out. He inspected the lookout station which he had installed a few years earlier and saw no damage. He returned to Mineral before dark. One his way back, he found a lost band of sheep and herded them back to Mineral to their owner. Can you imagine walking to the top of Lassen from Mineral through all that snow and ice in one day? There was no road at that time in the park.

Over the next several days, he led parties of newspaper reporters up the same route to take pictures of the eruptions. On the subsequent trips he discovered that the lookout house had been damaged, and he encountered an eruption while descending the mountain and lived through it.

Abbey retired officially from the Forest Service in 1920 but was still employed up to 1932. He was too good a man to lose. He left a diary of his service, which I am very thankful for. ☙

ARDITH

Mineral in the 1930s and 40s was a paradise for fishing and hunting. My father, Husky, took great advantage of where he lived. The limit for trout caught in the local streams was 25, and nobody had any trouble catching their limit. My father was a great fly fisherman, and he also loved to hunt deer. He had a hunting cabin on Turner Mountain and many friends and customers who accompanied him to it. The lookout and the cabin on Turner Mountain were about five miles from Mineral, but there was no road, so my father had 10 to 12 saddle horses for hunting and transportation to and from the cabin. They were pastured in Mineral in the summer and in Lanes Valley in the winter. As I remember, the horses were a mixed lot. New horses appeared from time to time. Some were hard to handle, but those that stayed a long time were pretty gentle. I remember one horse named Duster who was very easy riding on the downhill. Every hunter wanted him for the trip to Turner Mountain. How my father worked this out I am not sure.

When I was about 14, Ardith Wilson was hired as wrangler. She was to keep the horses saddled and ready for rental. She also acted as a guide. There couldn't have been a more perfect person for the job. Ardith was 16 and loved horses and the outdoors. She had grown up near Mineral, knew all sorts of wilderness lore, was an excellent artist, and could even yodel. At this point in time, my family lived in a house with five bedrooms, the original Hampton's home and hotel. Extra help lived with us, and Ardith was no exception. We had been in the Girl Scouts together and soon because fast friends. She was a very happy, friendly person, with deep blonde, wavy hair, always in blue jeans, and never without a smile.

To develop the horseback riding business, she needed trails to take the people on and insisted that I go with her as often as I could. I really did not like horses at all. My brother had been knocked off a horse when we were young and had a large scar on his arm from it, so I was very much afraid of horses. My father had given me a horse when I was five, and I had named it Margaret after my favorite cousin. It was a male horse and was later renamed Teddy. Needless to say, my father never gave me another horse.

I did, however, love the outdoors and was always eager for new experiences, so I did accompany Ardith a great deal of the time, but she had to saddle and bridle my horse. We found good trails that had been made by the Forest Service and other people. We rode to Magellan Lake and swam, to Turner Mountain and visited the person living in the lookout station, to Nanny Creek, to the Burn, and many other exciting places. One of our favorite places to go was Brokeoff Mountain. This was about eight miles from Mineral through the burn area where the brush was seven to eight feet tall along the trail, through beautiful Glassburner Meadows, and finally up to the side of Brokeoff. We would leave the horses tied to a tree and walk the last mile and a half to the top of the mountain. There is no more spectacular view of Lassen Peak than from this trail. You are slogging along on a steep slope. Suddenly there is a break and there, in all its glory, is this beautiful mountain that seems close enough to touch—Lassen Peak.

Ardith Wilson

We often helped the Forest Service supply the lookout station on Brokeoff by leading two loaded mules up to the top of the mountain. These lookout stations were a great aid in spotting forest fires and were operated during the fire season from June until the first rains in the fall. It was a lonely, solitary life, and it was always interesting to talk to the operator and learn how he or she ticked. It was a sad day for us when the National Park Service burned down the old Brokeoff lookout building after it was no longer used.

Ardith worked with the horses for six or seven years until she graduated from Chico State University. She taught physical education at the high school in Weaverville. She later married and had two sons who she was very proud of.

Several years ago, Ardith and I traveled together to Estes Park in Colorado to visit Emma Potts, the Girl Scout Leader we had in Mineral. Ardith had not changed—she had the same easy smile and never-grow-old attitude. She died a few years ago of Parkinson's disease. I miss her friendship, but I will always have the memories of the great times we had in Mineral riding the trails.

Girl Scout insignia (courtesy Joan Swartzlow McDougel)

Turner Mountain Lookout sketch by Ardith Wilson

Brokeoff Mountain sketch by Ardith Wilson

CCC warming hut in Lassen Park (courtesy Dan Foster)

CHAPTER 18

THE CCC CAMP

The Civilian Conservation Camp (CCC) was a program operated by the U. S. government beginning in 1933 and ending in 1942. Mineral had a CCC camp that operated during those years. It was situated across Highway 36 from the current CalTrans facility. Beginning in 1975, Al Schneider, Chief Ranger at Lassen Park, spent his spare time cleaning up the camp area so it could be used for a sports and picnic site. Locally it was christened "Schneider Stadium." It is still available for use for a small fee to the federal government.

The CCC program was one of the most popular and successful New Deal programs of President Franklin Roosevelt. It was designed to provide jobs for young men between the ages of 18-23, help their families financially, and aid in the conservation and development of natural resources in rural areas. During the nine years it existed, three million young men were enrolled, with a maximum of 300,000 at any one time. The men were provided with shelter, clothing, food, and a small wage of $30 a month, $25 of which was sent home to their families.

A large number of the CCC boys who were stationed in Mineral came from the southern part of the United States. Two of these made Mineral a permanent home later. Hugh Fields married a local Red Bluff girl and lived in Mineral for several years working for CalTrans. He was the first to see the 1949 Mineral Lodge fire. His children still live in the area. Thurmond Elliot worked as a summer ranger for Lassen Park while working on his teaching credential. He taught school in Taft, later building a summer home in Mineral. What I remember best about Elliot was the building of his summer home. He was his own designer and was greatly surprised to find that manufacturers did not make windows to fit the spaces he had left for them, so none of the windows in the house opened because he could only use plain glass. This house still stands at the end of Hampton Avenue. Both of these men came from rural Georgia.

Reserve officers from the U. S. Army were in charge of the camps, although there was no military training involved. But it is felt that the work and discipline in the camps enabled the quick mobilization of the United States for World War II. The program was enacted very quickly after legislation was signed on March 31, 1933. By July 1 of that same year, there were 1,473 working camps and a maximum of 2,900 camps by August of 1935.

The camps were located in areas where particular conservation was to be performed—in the case of Mineral, near Lassen Park. Each camp had up to 200 enrollees housed in structured barracks of 50 men each. Each camp was a temporary community in itself, supplying all the necessary personnel and support staff for the entire operation of the camp. Mineral's camp had its own doctor, which also helped out the local community. I remember going there for some ailment at one time. I also remember going there for a Thanksgiving or Christmas dinner. I was too young to know what work the CCC's did except the drainage ditches at the Lassen Park headquarters that were lined with beautiful rock work. Nationally, the CCC volunteers planted nearly three billion trees to help reforest America, constructed more than 800 parks nationwide, and upgraded other state and national parks. They also updated forest firefighting methods and built a network of service buildings and public roadways in remote areas.

The boys from the local CCC were a nightmare for my mother because she was the local postmaster. Each boy received five dollars per month that allowed them to order merchandise cash on delivery (C.O.D.) My mother had to store the boxes until the boys had enough money to pay the C.O.D. charges. Lots of times they never had enough money to bail out the package. I remember one time seeing a whole wall of boot boxes stacked as high as they would go and hearing my mother's exasperated sigh!

The legacy left by the Mineral CCC camp is Schneider Field and the numerous uses of the CCC barrack buildings. The Ski Hut at the Lassen Park Ski Area, which we operated from 1957 to 1967, was one of these buildings. Not great, but it kept us warm and dry all those years.

Interior of the ski hut that was the CCC warming hut, c. 1958 (courtesy Dan Foster)

LOST

I had always heard that anyone confused or lost in open country walks in a circle. Fortunately, this was the case of little Donny Metcalf, age five. The year was 1964, and my family owned and operated the Lassen Park Ski Area as well as Mineral Lodge. Thanks to the Bidstrup family who came from Sacramento, we had a large group of families who came to ski during Christmas vacation. This particular year, the Metcalf family of five children arrived before Christmas.

Behind the Lodge we owned land covered with trees, especially the white and red fir species that make great Christmas trees. This day, several families led by my brother, Fred, and my husband, George, trekked to the back land to cut trees for any family who was there for the holidays. This was a large group consisting of many children and several adults. Each family had a wonderful time selecting a tree, cutting the trees down, and taking them back to their respective cabin or motel room for decorating. They had been back at the Lodge for a short period when the Metcalfs realized that Donny was not with them or any of the other families.

This was December in the mountains, with the temperature around 20 degrees, and frozen snow on the ground. Hard snow does not show tracks. Donny was only five and small for his age. He was dressed in ski clothing, but his chances of survival were slim to none if they did not locate him before dark. You can well imagine the panic and fear in everyone's hearts, let alone the consequences if he was not found. His absence was discovered right before noon, so they had about five hours to find him. The weather was clear, which was a plus. The adult men returned to the tree cutting site, shouting his name, and looking for any clue. Donny wore a pair of boots with steel plates on the toes and heels that would fit the bindings on his skis. These steel plates made a dent in the hard snow. The men were able to locate his tracks heading west.

Fred and Donny's father followed the tracks for over three hours before they found the little boy asleep beside Battle Creek. He had completed almost half of the circle and was heading around east when they located him. He had crossed Highway 36, but continued on his circuitous route.

He could not get across Battle Creek because the water was deep and cold. What saved his life were the plates on the boots and Battle Creek. One can well imagine everyone's relief when he was found safe and sound.

Twenty years later, I was living in Sacramento selling commercial real estate. One evening, my friend Joan Tierny and I stopped to visit her married sister. The name Donny Metcalf was mentioned, and I wondered why the name sounded familiar. Later I found out that Joan's sister was married to the Donny Metcalf who had been lost in the woods of Mineral. Small world.

Mineral during winter, c. 1958

Gabriel "Minki" Brown

Wild Timber Lily

CHAPTER 19

MINKI

My friend Gabriel Brown, aka Minki, was 88 when she died. I have a hard time thinking of her as old because she was always so young in spirit.

Minki came to Mineral in her mid-twenties as a war bride. Her birthplace was Austria where she met and married Dick Brown from Westwood, California. Dick had been in the 10th Mountain Division in World War II where he managed an R&R Resort in the Austrian Alps. Minki was a ski instructor there. Mineral, being a small community where everyone knew everybody and everything, was excited to learn about her impending arrival. Her mother was a countess, so that made it even more interesting. I remember I was 15 and waiting tables in the Mineral Lodge Restaurant when I first saw Minki. I am not sure what I expected, but she looked more like the rugged outdoors type than a well-groomed daughter of a countess. And that was just what she was and a lot more.

Minki and I did not become good friends until several years later when I married and moved back to Mineral to operate Mineral Lodge and raise a family. But I had heard about her. According to local legend she was not an orthodox housekeeper or mother. She did not follow the "Ladies Home Companion" methods as the other local women did. They attributed this to her Austrian roots. Years later, when visiting her sister and family in Austria, I discovered that they blamed her different behavior on Americans. The truth was Minki just did it her way, a concept unheard of in the 1950s.

Minki loved to hike and to ski, both available for her in Mineral, and she was always pursuing these activities. My first big hike with her was from the Hole-in-the-Ground Campground to Black Rock on Mill Creek. She had discovered the trail on a map and wanted to try it as a day hike. It looked like about 20 miles to me, so I insisted on taking sleeping bags and enough food. It was a wonderful trip, but it took a good two days. The trip opened up a whole new world for Minki. She loved that canyon and all its lore of Ishi and the Mill Creek Indians. She spent a great deal of her time there, studying the Mill Creek canyon history and writing poetry that made her a prime speaker for historical events. It became a ritual of spring for us to hike that trail. I always looked forward to this trip, but I was also thankful to be home without encountering a rattlesnake. Diamondback rattlers were prevalent in that area.

Minki had four children, three girls and one boy. As they grew up, she decided to teach school. She had a BA degree from the University of Heidelberg so was given an equivalent degree from the University of California, along with a California Teaching Credential. She usually taught the lower grades in the Mineral School but was also the principal for most of her career. At that time, there were 40 or more students. Minki's classroom looked disorganized, but it was not. She was a wonderful teacher because she somehow motivated the students to perform at their highest level. They could not wait to get their assignments for the day. She taught all of my children and my nephews for all eight grades. Their education was not lacking, although she, again, was a trifle unorthodox in her methods. For a time, there was no substitute teacher available, so I performed this function with my university degree.

She went cross-country and downhill skiing as much as she could. She never left a stone unturned in anything that caught her interest. She was always taking long backpacking hikes with others, whenever she could. During the 1960 Olympics in Squaw Valley, Minki was hired as an interpreter for the German and Austrian ski teams. She spent a whole month there and loved every minute of it.

Minki was great fun to be with because her glass was always half-full, and she could not wait to fill it up. Her zest for life was infectious, and she added a lot to the community of Mineral. I took many hikes and trips with her, each of them filled with adventure and lots of laughter. She will always be in my heart with fond memories. Her home was filled with books and pictures of her many interests, her paintings, and poetry.

Minki suffered great tragedy in a six months period: Her husband died of a heart attack, her youngest daughter was killed in an auto accident, and her mother passed away in Austria. Her great faith in God, and her teaching responsibilities, enabled her to move through this tragic period of her life with no emotional scars. She was always concerned about the American Indians, so when she retired from teaching, she spent two or three years on a Zuni Indian reservation. It did not sound like fun to me, but she loved it.

Her last years were spent taking care of her alcoholic son. By the time he died at 60, she had jeopardized her health and independence and was forced to live with her daughters and in convalescent homes. True to her nature, she kept a cheerful attitude and was always talking of new ideas.

She always planned to write this book about Mineral, but when she lost all her collected information that could not be replaced, she lost interest. I have written this book in her memory and for her. ☙

Jo Ann Beresford Perkins

Jo Ann Beresford Perkins graduated from Red Bluff High School and attended the University of California at Berkeley, graduating with a degree in Social Welfare.

She worked as a flight attendant in Denver, Colorado, for United Air Lines before her marriage to George Perkins. They returned to Mineral, operating Lassen Park Ski Area and the Mineral Lodge with her family until 1980.

Moving to Red Bluff as a real estate broker, she owned Mountain Valley Real Estate, the Victorian Restaurant, and worked as a tour director for Lassen Transit. She still owns a cabin in Mineral and lives in Northern California.